STRATEGY AND TACTICS
INFANTRY WARFARE

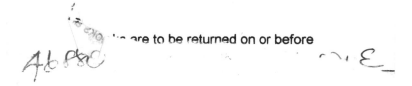

STRATEGY AND TACTICS
INFANTRY WARFARE

ANDREW WIEST AND M. K. BARBIER

This edition first published in 2002 by
MBI Publishing Company,
Galtier Plaza, Suite 200
380 Jackson Street
St. Paul, MN 55101 USA
www.motorbooks.com

MBI Publishing Company books are also available at discounts in bulk quantity
for industrial or sales-promotional use. For details write to Special Sales Manager
at Motorbooks International Wholesalers & Distributors, Galtier Plaza,
Suite 200, 380 Jackson Street, St. Paul, MN 55101 USA.

Library of Congress Cataloging-in-Publication Data available.

ISBN 0-7603-1401-2

Editorial and design by
Amber Books Ltd
Bradley's Close,
74–77 White Lion Street,
London N1 9PF

Project Editor: Charles Catton
Editor: Charlotte Rundall
Design: Neil Rigby at www.stylus-design.com
Picture Research: Lisa Wren and Chris Bishop

Printed and bound in Italy by: Eurolitho S.p.A., Cesano Boscone (MI)

Picture credits
All pictures supplied by **TRH Pictures**, except the following:
Aerospace Publishing: 15, 41, 44, 46, 47, 50, 72, 73, 75 (b).
US Department of Defense: 156–157, 158, 159, 162, 164, 165, 166, 167, 170(b), 172 (both), 173.

Artworks:
Peter Harper & Tony Randall

CONTENTS

CHAPTER ONE

INDUSTRIAL WAR

In the killing fields of World War I, the role of the infantry underwent a change that marked the birth of modern war. Troops who had gone into battle in line now had to cope with machine guns, aircraft and artillery.

Organized warfare has been a part of human experience since the dawn of civilization. Indeed the frequency of conflict seems to suggest that war is integral to the very nature of mankind. Political régimes rise and fall, the fortunes of religions ebb and flow, cultural values continually alter, but war remains. From the first war in the desert wastes of ancient Mesopotamia to the present war on terror, conflict has been a constant in the development of humankind.

Within the history of warfare, much has changed over the millennia. When Achilles battled Hector before the gates of Troy, wars were small and personal, involving hand-to-hand combat and individual physical prowess. Modern wars are technological wonders based on the military dominance of the microchip. Nearly invisible stealth aircraft can launch attacks using terminally guided munitions that strike their targets with laser-guided precision. Though technological advances, from the introduction of gunpowder to satellite targeting, have altered the manner in which war is prosecuted, in many ways the battlefield remains unchanged by history. War remains the domain where the violent, and all too often short life of the infantryman takes centre stage.

LEFT: Infantrymen from around the world gather in Peking (now Beijing) after the suppression of the Boxer Rebellion at the turn of the 20th century. At that time, military theorists of all nations were certain that the cold steel and spirit of the infantry would prove decisive in future conflicts.

ABOVE: British troops move forward in a clearing operation in the Brandwater area during the Boer War. Few European military leaders took note of the lessons learned in South Africa when laying their plans for what they believed would be decisive victory in World War I.

Throughout history military pundits have often readied the obituary of infantry warfare, predicting that armoured knights, gunpowder, rifled weapons, machine guns, tanks, aircraft, nuclear weapons and finally computers would make the infantryman obsolete. From the Greek phalanx to modern special forces, though, the infantry has done what it does best and fought on, sometimes against all odds. Though technological advances have increased the role of other services in wartime it remains the infantry that takes and holds land in battle. It also remains the infantry that suffers the bulk of the military casualties during conflicts.

Much has changed, but in the end, it is still the 'grunt' that fights and wins wars. Infantry defended Rome and destroyed Carthage, infantry won and lost the Napoleonic Wars, infantry suffered and died at Verdun, infantry overthrew Berlin, infantry fought a ragged war in the tunnels of the Viet Cong, and infantry routs terrorists from their mountain fastness. The methods of war have changed, but the infantry remains Queen of the Battlefield.

THE ROAD TO WORLD WAR I

Military history in the modern era has focused on the martial fortunes of the powerful nation states of Europe. Reaping the rewards of the Industrial Revolution and world-wide economic dominance, the nations of Europe towered over the remainder of the world in military strength in the 19th century.

After having spent a good deal of their latent energy fighting each other, in the wake of the Crimean War the nations of Europe began to turn their power upon the remainder of the world, embarking on a period of colonialism that would soon see great swaths of the globe under the suzerainty of European overlords. The typical view of colonial warfare contends that European armies, utilizing the military inventions of the Industrial Revolution, were able to run roughshod over outmatched native forces. Indeed some colonial wars did follow this pattern, including an easy defeat by the British of a massive Dervish force during 1898 at Omdurman.

However, when properly armed and led, native forces were able to score significant victories, including the Ethiopian defeat of the Italians. In perhaps the most revealing colonial conflict, the mighty British Empire had to struggle for years to overcome the stubborn guerrilla resistance of an irregular force in the Boer War. Though warning signs were evident, European nations emerged from the period of colonial warfare confident that their modern militaries could overcome all resistance, making modern warfare quick and decisive.

Several other conflicts also indicated that warfare in the age of the Industrial Revolution would be different from what most nations expected. The American Civil War had been anything but quick and decisive as the outgunned South managed to resist the seemingly inevitable Northern victory for nearly five years. Though the war included manoeuvre and quick victories, such as Lee's masterpiece at Chancellorsville, in the end it got bogged down. It became a war of sieges and a Northern constriction of the Southern will to fight, finally developing into what some historians consider to be the first total war.

The Prussian victories over Austria and France, on the surface, seemed to bode well for the concept of decisive war. Inept Austrian and French commanders should receive much of the blame for the quick defeat of their respective nations. Yet after the German victory over French forces at Sedan in 1870, the surrender of Napoleon III and the seeming collapse of France, the war lingered on. Many within the French population rose up and engaged in a guerrilla war against the increasingly frustrated Prussian military.

It was the Russo-Japanese War, though, that should have alarmed complacent European military theorists. Though the conflict is best known for decisive Japanese naval victories, it was decided by battle between massed infantry formations. The Battle of Mukden presaged the future, involving over 600,000 soldiers on a front of over 40 miles (64km) in a massive struggle that lasted for two weeks.

TOWARDS TOTAL WAR

Thus several conflicts indicated that future wars would not be decisive in nature, but would instead become attritional. Some military men, led by the Polish war theorist Jan Bloch, predicted that the next European conflict would be long and inconclusive. Most military men, believing implicitly in the dominance of the weaponry provided by the Industrial Revolution, remained confident in their belief that audacious attack would lead to lightning victories. Their faith in the wonders of the new weaponry, though, was misplaced.

The Industrial Revolution had changed the very nature of warfare, ushering in the era of modern, total war. Economic powerhouses, the nations of Europe were now able to raise and equip armies numbering in the millions, and keep them in the field for nearly five years. Thus the coming cataclysm would pit nation against nation rather than army against army, in a war that would achieve

BELOW: A Boer Commando in action in the Transvaal. Through the use of marksmanship and mounted mobility, the Boers were able to hold out against the much more powerful British Imperial forces for nearly three years.

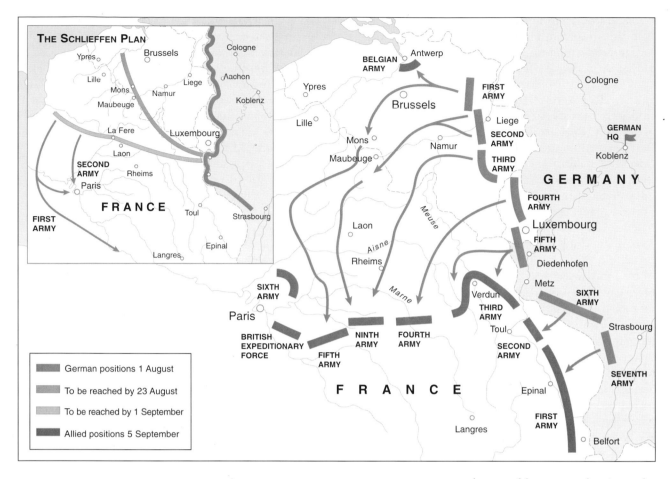

THE SCHLIEFFEN PLAN

German positions 1 August

To be reached by 23 August

To be reached by 1 September

Allied positions 5 September

ABOVE: A German machine gun company moves forward through the Argonne forest early on during World War I. The defensive power of weapons like the MG 08s seen here would become a major factor in infantry tactics to come.

complete victory or utter defeat. It was the factories of Europe and the years of accumulated wealth that made such a conflict possible. The effects of the Industrial Revolution also significantly altered the array of weaponry available to the combatants, having a direct effect on the tactical prosecution of battle. The infantry now carried bolt-action magazine rifles instead of the muzzle-loading smoothbores of old. Though the advance in weaponry made the infantry a more lethal force than ever before, it would be two other new weapons

systems that would come to dominate the battlefields during the Great War, and they were the quick-firing artillery piece and the machine gun.

Perfected by Hiram Maxim in 1883, the machine gun utilized the recoil generated by firing one shot to load the next shell. By the outset of the World War I machine guns were able to fire nearly 600 rounds per minute. War was now mechanized and technological, allowing machine guns to fill the air of the battlefield with deadly steel. Though it is difficult for the modern layman to understand, the generals of the Great War were slow to recognize the revolutionary nature of the machine gun. It had proven deadly in recent conflicts, but most military leaders were unable to admit that the machine gun could replace the fire of carefully trained marksmen. Most believed that in the coming conflict, the machine gun would cause heavy losses, but would prove merely to be an adjunct to the strength of advancing infantry, and they placed a higher value on discipline and military spirit. As it happens, the machine gun would prove more valuable in a defensive role. Working in tandem, the guns, mounted on tripods, could traverse back and forth utilizing interlocking zones of fire to produce a 'beaten zone' that would devastate an infantry force in the open.

DEFENSIVE DOMINANCE

Industrial advances in metallurgy and high explosives also transformed the role of artillery in the Great War. In most previous wars, artillery pieces had aimed over open sights using direct fire. However, stronger barrels and higher muzzle velocities had greatly increased the range of artillery by 1914. In addition, recoil-absorbing devices obviated the need to re-aim artillery pieces after each shot. Finally, the use of high explosive over black powder increased the lethality of each artillery shell. Simply put, artillery could now outrange and outgun the infantry. Firing from miles behind the lines, artillery – including the famous French 75mm (2.95in) field gun, which could fire up to 15 rounds per minute – could decimate attacking infantry forces. Utilizing a frightening array of air-burst shrapnel shells and high explosives, artillery, especially when used in tandem with machine guns, could rain a 'storm of steel' upon any attacker. This new weaponry was destined to make the Great War a struggle in which the defensive dominated, calling for dramatic changes in the tactics used by attacking infantry. To the gentlemen amateur officers of turn-of-the-century militaries, though, such changes were anathema.

For numerous reasons, most military theorists at the turn of the century believed that future conflicts would be quick and decisive in nature. It seemed that modern economies were so interconnected and that industrial war would be so expensive that no nation could stand the strain of war for a long period. Also, the grievous losses inflicted by modern weaponry would force national collapses quicker than ever before. All across Europe military commanders, then, came to believe that the best method to win the coming war was through massive, audacious attack forcing an enemy surrender, and the 'Cult of the Offensive' was born. As war neared, each of the major European powers readied their offensive plans: the Germans had the Schlieffen Plan, the French had Plan 17 and the Russians

had Plan 19. Though they varied in their particulars, the attack plans were all based on the same concept: the war would be won through superior fighting spirit, or what the French called élan; it would be the army that persevered psychologically in the face of heavy losses that would achieve victory; training and discipline would force the infantry through the 'storm of steel'; and only through attacking would their morale be kept high, leading to ultimate victory.

Though much of the planning and staff work that went into the opening phases of World War I was quite detailed – especially the logistical support of the German Schlieffen Plan that called for an massive envelopment of the entire French Army – infantry tactics were rudimentary and essentially linear in nature. Relying in the main on brute force and spirit after a period of manoeuvring, opposing forces planned to meet in battle in thick skirmish lines. With their attendant machine guns and artillery relegated to a supporting role, the massive lines of infantry would blaze away at each other in a great test of wills. The conclusion would come as the morale of one of the forces broke, after which the victors would charge forward with fixed bayonets in order to administer the death blow. Finally, the cavalry forces would gallop in to harry the defeated and retreating foe. In military academies across Europe, officers learned their lessons. World War I would follow a four-step pattern: manoeuvre, locking in battle, the wearing-down fight and, finally, the exploitation.

OPPOSITE: The pre-war Schlieffen Plan for the invasion of Belgium and France, compared with the actual progress of Germany's attack, in which the right wing failed to encircle Paris.

BELOW: After the failure of great offensives in 1914, the combatants on the Western Front began to dig in. The creation of the trench systems would transform the conflict into a bloody four-year stalemate.

Even as the great military minds of Europe dreamed of quick victory, the abilities of modern weaponry available at the time had already tipped the balance of the war to the defensive. There were also some technological shortcomings that worked against the attacker. The battlefields of World War I would be vast, making command and control very difficult. Communications technology, in the form of the telegraph and the telephone, enabled defenders to react with great speed. However, attacking forces had to rely on runners or carrier pigeons to receive their information. Radios were still in their infancy and telephonic communications were too vulnerable. In short, military leaders had little control over their attacking forces once they left their start line. Defenders, though, could react to a changing situation much more quickly. In addition, attackers in the Great War lacked a weapon of exploitation. Cavalry – the weapon of choice in previous wars – proved too vulnerable to the 'storm of steel'. Armour – the weapon of choice in later wars – was not yet up to the task. Thus attackers moved forward only at the pace of marching soldiers. Defenders, though, could utilize lateral rail lines and road communications to shift forces. Simply put, the defenders of World War I could think and react more quickly than the attackers. Thus all of the initial advantages in the war lay with the defender, but every combatant planned to rely on the strength of the attack. It would be the infantry that paid the price.

THE OUTBREAK OF WAR

In 1914 the nations of Europe stood ready to unleash a cataclysm of war like the world had never seen. It was the titanic clash of arms on the Western Front that would come to represent the epitome of modern, total war and would revolutionize the nature of combat. The French Army, under the command of General Joseph Joffre, numbered some two million men and was augmented by the strength of the 150,000-man British Expeditionary Force (BEF). Following the dictates of the 'Cult of the Offensive' the mighty French force, under the operational orders of Plan 17, attacked eastwards into Alsace and Lorraine. Massed infantry formations, supported by quick-firing 75s and relying on élan, moved forward in linear fashion. Sheer numbers and willpower would be able to overcome the strength of the German defences in the area.

The Germans, in turn, fielded a force of some three million men under the command of General Hemuth von Moltke. German planners realized that the French would attempt to attack into Alsace and Lorraine, states lost to Germany at the close of the Franco-Prussian War, and hoped to use the predictability of the French plan to their advantage. The Schlieffen Plan, developed by Chief of the German General Staff

RIGHT: Soldiers from the Australian and New Zealand Army Corps, or ANZAC, forces rush forward into the attack at Gallipoli. Most military leaders of the time erroneously believed that the spirit, or élan, of attacking infantry could overcome massed defensive firepower, leading to decisive victory.

Alfred von Schlieffen, called for only a weak defence in Alsace-Lorraine. The weakness of the defence in this area would lull the French into complacency and lure their forces forward away from their bases of communication. As the French advanced, the bulk of the German forces would wheel through Belgium and into lightly defended northern France. Thus as the French moved forward, the Germans would pivot through northern France, envelop Paris, and attack the French forces in the south from behind. Rather like a revolving door, as the French pushed in Alsace-Lorraine, the German 'door' would hit them in the back. Thus Moltke hoped to prosecute a battle of envelopment, thereby surrounding and destroying the entire French Army in less than six weeks.

Initially the Schlieffen Plan worked to perfection as German infantry thundered through Belgium and nearly enveloped the valiant BEF on 23 and 24 August at the Battle of Mons. Unaware of the threat, Joffre continued with Plan 17, against stronger than expected German resistance. Circumstances and the nature of infantry warfare in 1914, though, soon conspired to tip the balance of the campaign against the Germans. Shaken and unnerved by the pressure of command, Moltke committed several basic military errors. He altered the Schlieffen Plan and strengthened the defensive forces in Alsace-Lorraine, both weakening his attacking forces and

preventing the French from being drawn forward. Also, frightened by an expected Russian attack into Germany, Moltke further weakened his attacking forces by shifting men to the Eastern Front. Though German forces were still advancing on schedule, the weakened attackers began to slow, and the delicate logistic support required for such a massive operation began to falter.

At nearly the same time, General Joffre belatedly realized the threat posed by the German advance, and called a halt to Plan 17. Seemingly unperturbed by events, he began the task of shifting his massive army northwards to meet the developing

ABOVE: Australian troops at Gallipoli demonstrate some of the improvisations forced on infantrymen by the nature of the Great War. The soldier on the right peers over the edge of the trench with the aid of a periscope, while the man in the centre uses a sniperscope to fire while remaining in safety.

ABOVE: Canadian troops of the 87th Battalion resting in a trench near Willerval. For the ordinary infantryman, trench warfare was rarely better than miserable. In fact, most of the time his life was little more than a squalid and exhausting existence.

quickly than the Germans could advance. The sheer numbers of the French Army and the resilience of a modern nation at war had served to blunt the effect of the continuing string of German victories, successes that might have been decisive in earlier wars. Even with the advantages of surprise and numbers, the German attackers had suffered grievously at the hands of small forces utilizing massed defensive firepower. Thus as September approached, the balance in the north shifted. The Allies now had 41 divisions in the area, while German forces, undersupplied and weakened by exertion, numbered only 25 divisions.

BATTLE OF THE MARNE

On 6 September French and British forces near Paris attacked the flank of the German advance, launching the Battle of the Marne. Far behind the lines and confused by events, Moltke had lost control of the situation, and after a confused, see-saw battle, the Germans chose to retreat to defensive positions along the Aisne River and began to dig in. On 14 November, hoping to score a great victory, Joffre's forces attacked the sketchy German defensive lines along the Chemin des Dames Ridge. Though outnumbered, the Germans, utilizing the defensive prowess of machine guns and artillery, defeated the French advances with relative ease. Searching for an open flank, both the Germans and the Allies began to advance northward in a period of the war called 'the Race to the Sea'. Though the Germans once again attacked the depleted BEF in the savage encounter known as the Battle of First Ypres, the defensive lines once again held. By the end of the year the battle lines had been drawn from the English Channel to Switzerland, and both sides began to construct trench systems. The Great War on the Western Front had become a stalemate, a stalemate running the length of France and involving millions of combatants and the economic outputs of entire nations. The nature of the war had changed. There would be no quick, decisive victory, for the infantry had proven unable to overcome the defensive 'storm of steel'.

German threat to the city of Paris. Utilizing lateral rail lines, Joffre was able to move his forces northwards, reconfiguring his defensive alignments much more quickly than the Germans could advance on foot. In addition, though they had moved from victory to victory, the German infantry had suffered greatly at the hands of the outnumbered Allied forces. Concentrated rifle, machine gun and artillery fire had served to blunt several German assaults, allowing the BEF to escape destruction at Mons and Le Cateau. With their armies weakened and falling behind schedule, the Germans chose to wheel inside of Paris to save time. It was a critical error, offering the flank of the German advance to French forces massing in defence of their capital. The reality of infantry warfare had tipped the tactical balance. The French had been able to react on the defensive more

Across the length of France, both the Germans and the Allies had dug in, hoping to recuperate from their losses, marshal their forces and attack again. Trained for open warfare and yearning for decisive victory, military leaders on both sides originally paid scant attention to their developing defensive lines, but it would be trenches that would come to dominate the remainder of the conflict, and it would be trenches that changed the very nature of warfare.

At first the opposing defensive lines were rudimentary, meant only to hold until the resumption of offensive, manoeuvre warfare. Within a few months, though, the defensive lines were becoming more and more complex, taking on an air of permanence. The trenches themselves, constructed in a defensive zigzag pattern, were usually 8ft (2.4m) deep, honeycombed with large and small underground dugouts that kept their occupants safe from all but a direct hit from a heavy-calibre artillery shell. From the front-line trench, communications trenches led back towards the rear to second- and third-line defensive trenches. Within the trench systems, natural defensive features were converted into redoubts. As a result trench systems in World War I were extensive, often forming confusing rabbit warrens of interlocking defensive emplacements, sometimes of up to 24km (36.8 miles) in extent.

The complicated, nearly invulnerable, trench lines bristled with defensive firepower. Impassable forests of barbed-wire entanglements, thigh-high and sometimes nearly 40m (44yd) in depth, guarded the front-line trench. In addition to the rifle fire of the trench occupants, machine guns located in highly defended nests and utilizing interlocking zones of fire – stood ready to defend the trenches with countless million rounds of fire. Further to the rear the quick-firing and deadly artillery of the Great War, already sighted in on their targets, were able to cover attackers with a steel rain of high explosive and deadly shrapnel. Thus the defensive works of World War I were quite complicated and quite deadly, much more so than the modern-day military commander, aided by a vast array of new offensive weaponry, could understand.

BELOW: Over the Top! British soldiers emerge from their trenches to move forward into no-man's-land. Survival was often a matter of chance in the face of enemy artillery and machine guns, but the Great War added a new horror, poison gas, which was used on an large scale for the first time.

The Great War had settled down into a massive stalemate on the Western Front, though in Russia and in other far-flung theatres the conflict remained more fluid in nature. Commanders in the West began to wrestle with a problem that seemingly defied solution. Wars are, in the main, won by attacking. How, then, were attackers to overcome the defensive works of their enemy and achieve the long-awaited decisive victory?

The Germans, under their new commander Erich von Falkenhayen, chose to stand on the defensive in the West while concentrating their efforts against the Russians. It was, then, the Allies who would spend 1915 in search of answers to the riddle of trench warfare. In a series of battles spanning much of the Western Front, including the Battle of Neuve Chapelle, it became apparent to most Allied commanders, including Joffre and General Sir Douglas Haig – who would soon take command of the BEF – that it would not be infantry tactics that would reign supreme during the Great War.

The infantryman, armed with his rifle and bayonet, could do but little against an enemy in trenches guarded by barbed wire and defended by machine guns and artillery. The infantry was too vulnerable and carried too little firepower to have a meaningful effect on the outcome of the coming battles. Though some retained hope of its usefulness, the cavalry too proved to be of little value against an entrenched foe. Nor were machine guns, powerful but not yet portable, the answer for those seeking offensive victory. In the end it became obvious to most that the only weapon in the attacker's arsenal that was capable of defeating these defensive trench systems was artillery.

It, too, had a hidden flaw. Firing from miles behind the lines and using indirect fire, for the first time artillery had to be able to hit what it could not see. Trenches, dug-outs and machine gun nests are – especially from 11 miles (17.6km) away – small targets which require direct hits to ensure their destruction. Simply put, the artillerists of the Great War did not yet posses the technical expertise or the communications technology to achieve such accuracy. During this phase of World War I, artillery could destroy large targets, such as massed infantry attempting to cross no man's land, but was not yet able to strike particular targets that it could not see. Even so, it would be artillery that would come to dominate much of the offensive action of the Great War.

THE SOMME

During 1916 on the Western Front both the Germans and the British sought to score decisive victories aimed at shattering the opposing trench systems and thereby restoring a war of movement. Both commanders, Falkenhayen and Haig, relied on the dominance of artillery to achieve their proposed victories, sparing only scant thought for the tactics of their massive, but outmatched, infantry formations. The resulting struggles at Verdun and the Somme would become the signature battles of the Great War, in the main giving the conflict its reputation for futile slaughter. Perhaps the greatest single

BELOW: British soldiers examine the sighting mechanism of an American-built Browning machine gun. Such weapons, able to fire over 750 rounds per minute, meant that the time-honoured tactic of advancing in line abreast had become suicidal. Even so, it took commanders several years and millions of lives to realize that fact.

battle of World War I, Verdun lasted from 21 February to 18 December, claiming over 800,000 casualties in a horrific battle of attrition designed to break the French will to fight. Falkenhayen hoped to pit German steel against French flesh, calling down a hailstorm of artillery fire upon the defenders of the embattled city. In many ways, though, it was the Battle of the Somme that best illustrates the state of warfare existing in 1916.

The British, having raised their first truly mass army, hoped to use their newfound might to rupture the German defensive system near the River Somme, partly in an effort to aid their embattled ally. The commander of the BEF, General Haig, planned to win victory at the Somme through sheer weight of artillery fire. Towards this end, the BEF gathered together some 1400 artillery pieces and countless millions of artillery shells. Victory would rest upon the efforts of but one branch of the armed forces. The artillery had to flatten the German barbed wire, destroy the German trench system as well as its inhabitants, and finally silence the German artillery. The infantry would simply advance in the wake of the pulverizing barrage and occupy the shattered and defenceless German trenches. Advancing shoulder to shoulder in waves, the infantry would walk across no man's land, using discipline, courage and the strength of sheer numbers to overcome any German defensive fire that remained. Thus at this stage of World War I, infantry tactics harked back to the linear tactics used in the days of Frederick the Great. Artillery had become the queen of battle, leaving the infantry as its adjunct.

On 24 June 1916 the British artillery launched its hurricane of fire, beginning a week-long bombardment in which some one-and-a-half million shells rained down on the German trenches. Though the bombardment was quite impressive, and convinced many of the British soldiers that nobody in the German trenches would emerge alive, the barrage failed to achieve any of its main goals. Around 1000 of the guns that took part in the bombardment were field guns, which were not powerful enough either to destroy trenches or duel with German artillery. In addition, nearly a million of the shells fired in the bombardment were

air-burst shrapnel shells, effective against exposed targets but of little value against trenches and dug-outs. Thus only 400 artillery pieces firing 500,000 shells were assigned to do the bulk of the damage, not nearly enough to complete the task. Also, since Britain's industry had only recently begun shell making, 30 per cent of the shells used in the bombardment were faulty, possibly even duds. Finally, given the inaccuracy of indirect fire, only 2 shells in every 100 were direct hits; the others were loud but ineffective.

ABOVE: British soldiers firing a Lewis Gun, a truly portable machine gun, which would serve to strengthen the role of attacking infantry.

BELOW: German infantry training for trench raids. Clubs, bayonets, pistols and other close-combat weapons were ideal for the vicious man-to-man fighting typical of the trenches.

ABOVE: A British soldier peers warily out into no-mans-land through his trench periscope. Trench raids were a constant threat as both sides sent out intelligence-gathering patrols, whose aim was to capture prisoners who could be grilled during interrogation.

As a result, when the bombardment ceased, though frightened, most of the German defenders were very much alive as the British infantry went 'over the top', dressed their lines and began walking towards their foe. The Germans readied their machine guns and artillery and called down the storm of steel. Though gallant, the British attackers, armed in the main with rifles, could do little against such defensive firepower and an entrenched enemy. Only on the southern portion of the front did the British infantry make substantial gains, while along most other parts of the line, they did not even reach the German front-line trenches. The effort to achieve a crushing victory through weight of artillery fire had failed, and nearly 57,000 British soldiers had fallen in a single day. As a result, the Battle of the Somme settled down into a six-month struggle of attrition that eventually claimed one million casualties. Though the British made alterations to their offensive schemes, including the introduction of the tank, the reality of the Great War remained unchanged. The defenders were still able to out-think and outperform their attackers. Much would have to change to tip the balance of futility.

TECHNOLOGICAL CHANGES

Many historians and military history aficionados fail to look much past the Somme in their study of the Great War. The remainder of the conflict seems to be a great mass of trench struggles representing the height of military stupidity and a dearth of tactical development. Victory came only after years of attrition, the introduction of fresh American soldiers and the onset of revolution. The truth is, as usual, much more complicated than this.

The years 1917 and 1918 in fact represent a sea change in modern warfare, and a compressed period of tactical innovation rarely seen. During a period that many Great War historians simply call 'the Learning Curve', commanders on both sides of the front lines began to rethink the very nature of modern warfare. As a result, technological changes and tactical innovations would come to solve the riddle of the dominance of the defensive. Warfare shifted dramatically, from being a 'great game', practised by gentlemen amateurs, to being technical and tactical, practised by the first generation of true professionals. War, now industrial and total, had entered the 20th century and had become modern.

Revealing the complete reliance upon the nation in total war, many of the changes that would alter the Great War were advances made by scientists and engineers rather than by military men. Where in 1916 infantry had been nearly powerless against an entrenched foe, new inventions by 1918 had once again made the infantry powerful. The best-known such invention was the tank, but it was, in some ways, at the time the least important. Lightly armed and slow-moving, the tank was in its infancy, and though it would prove a valuable adjunct it was not yet a dominant weapon of war.

It was the more mundane developments that made the infantry powerful, enabling it to work with the other arms of the military and restore balance and movement to the battlefield. New, portable machine guns – including the famous British Lewis gun – added to the infantry's firepower. In addition, the infantry now had its own portable artillery in the form of modern hand grenades and mortars. This new

weaponry enabled the infantry to deal with defensive emplacements on its own, rather than having to wait for artillery support. In addition, the infantry also possessed other, more case-specific weaponry, including bangalore torpedoes and the intimidating flamethrowers.

Other technological developments served to help bring the various components of the modern military into closer battlefield harmony. Military aircraft which, like the tank, would come to revolutionize war, saw significant action in the Great War, but had their greatest value in a reconnaissance role. Coupled with advances in aerial photography and radio communications, aircraft were able by 1918 accurately to locate enemy defensive works and serve as artillery spotters, heralding a military communications revolution that is embodied today by the microchip.

Scientific developments more specific to artillery also began to tip the balance in favour of the attacker. In 1916 artillery could not hit what it could not see. By 1918 much had been learned about the effects of barrel wear and weather on shell trajectory. Techniques known as 'flash spotting' and 'sound ranging' were able to pinpoint the location of enemy artillery pieces. Aerial photography had provided artillerists with accurate maps of

OPPOSITE: A German soldier hurls a hand grenade over a barbed-wire entanglement in 1917. Along with the light machine gun, grenades became a vital tool for the World War I infantryman during the bitter, short-range combat in the trenches, helping clear trenches of enemy opposition.

BELOW: An Austrian trench mortar fires against Italian forces in the rugged, mountainous terrain of the Italian Front. This simple weapon gave infantry units their own short-range fire support, and it could be used to drop mortar bombs directly into enemy trenches.

OPPOSITE: British and French troops react to an air attack on the Western Front. Air power had little direct effect on ground troops early on in the war, but by 1918 the development of effective ground-attack aircraft made antiaircraft – or, as it was popularly called by pilots, 'Ack-Ack' – weaponry much more important.

BELOW: German troops moving forward on the Isonzo Front in Italy. Abandoning the tactic of advancing in waves, the Germans had developed the so-called 'Hutier' Tactics, named after the commander of the Eighteenth Army where they were first used. Also called 'Infiltration' or 'Stormtrooper' tactics, the new system called for infantry to rush forward in small units, making best use of cover.

enemy defences. When coupled with relentless on-the-job training such technological advances had transformed the power of artillery. By 1918 artillery was able to hit what it could not see with deadly accuracy, with no preregistration. Thus trenches and dug-outs were no longer safe havens of defence. In barely two years of innovation, artillery had become modern – a science and no longer an art – establishing practices which are still prevalent today.

As the balance of the war began to shift, military leaders in every combatant nation struggled to develop tactics that – utilizing the new weaponry – would bring the longed-for victory. Though all sides experimented in their offensive tactics, it is the Germans who usually receive credit for updating the old, linear system and thus showing the way forward into modern war.

Having witnessed daring new Russian infantry tactics on the Eastern Front, General Oskar Hutier began to codify a new attack formula that would come to bear his name. His tactical scheme called for the newly powerful infantry to advance in wedge formations and in short bursts rather than in slow, ponderous waves. Highly trained élite soldiers, referred to as storm troops, would lead the assault. With their new firepower and communications abilities the storm troops would probe the enemy lines for weak points.

Once located, the troops could use their own weaponry to achieve a breech in the line, with the goal of advancing to tactical depth. No longer was it necessary to attempt to overthrow the entire enemy defensive system utilizing the brute force of great numbers. The quickly advancing storm troops would attempt to disrupt the enemy defensive system by striking at supporting artillery and command centres. In many ways the new style of warfare was *Blitzkrieg* without tanks. The enemy defences were now seen as a system. It was the job of the storm troops to short-circuit the brain of the system rather than to batter the body. Though the Germans were the first to codify 'Hutier Tactics', they had learned much of the way forward from Russian innovations, ones that would become very important in the World War II and the Cold War. At the same time the Western Allies were also moving along the learning curve, readying their own advanced tactics for 1918.

THE BIRTH OF MODERN WARFARE

The fighting on the Western Front in 1918 – all too often ignored by military historians – represents the culmination of a revolutionary period in the history of warfare. A far cry from the blundering, gentlemen amateurs of 1914, the military practitioners of 1918 laid the foundations for every war since. Blitzkrieg, Soviet Deep Battle and even Coalition forces in

the Gulf War trace their origins back to the Western Front at the close of the Great War. In four short years, warfare had come of age.

The Germans, under the command of General Paul von Hindenburg and his Chief of Staff General Erich von Ludendorff, unleashed their new style of warfare on 21 March 1918 in a last, desperate bid to achieve total victory. The surprised men of the British 5th Army suffered greatly in the assault, very nearly breaking. With the aid of an accurate artillery bombardment, dubbed a 'fire waltz', German forces advanced nearly 7 miles (11km) before nightfall, an unheard-of development for the Great War. By 6 April the Germans had advanced nearly 40 miles (64.3km), and victory seemed to beckon.

At this point, however, the realities of the Great War intervened. As Joffre had before, Haig and General Philippe Pétain, the new French commander, were able to rush reinforcements to the scene more quickly than the now-exhausted Germans could advance on foot. Thus the Allied lines finally held, leaving the Germans to defend a vulnerable salient having suffered over 200,000 casualties, a total that they could ill afford after nearly

five years of war. Undaunted, the Germans went on to launch a further series of offensives, leading to very similar results and culminating in the Second Battle of the Marne. Thus the Germans had proven the strength of their new tactics, but were still unable to solve the overall riddle of trench warfare.

The Allies had also been experimenting with new tactics, as evidenced by the first massed use of tanks in the Battle of Cambrai in November 1917. Even as the

ABOVE: The arrival of the US Army in 1918 brought new strength to the Allied cause. These members of the 369th Regiment, 93rd Division – one of two segregated 'Colored' Divisions in France – are seen in the Argonne region on 4 May 1918.

ABOVE: A line of Renault FT-17 light tanks creeps through the French countryside near the end of the Great War. Although the tank was far from being a war-winning weapon at this stage, it had an immense psychological effect on defending infantry, and far-sighted pioneers were already thinking about how it should be used in future. It was the basis for the Russian T-series of tanks, the most widely produced of which was the famous T-34.

Germans attacked, the British were planning to put their new tactics to the test yet again. Even more so than the Germans, the British planned to use unprecedented levels of all-arms coordination during their coming offensive, giving each facet of the military its role to play in a resounding, harmonious symphony of war.

The artillery, which had been called upon to win battles in 1916, was to prepare the way. Accurate and powerful, the artillery had only to keep the Germans under cover during the infantry advance. Using the new infiltration tactics the British infantry would then advance to depth, accompanied by over 400 lumbering tanks, a weapons system that the Germans had virtually ignored. Though the tanks would not be decisive, they could deal with enemy strongpoints and machine-gun nests. Overhead, Allied air superiority would communicate the progress of the battle to the other facets of the military, as well as engage in a ground-attack role in order to interdict any enemy movement. Much had changed since the stalemate trench-warfare tactics of 1916.

The British forces, aided by the arrival of masses of American troops and a slow decline in German morale, on 8 August rushed forward into the Battle of Amiens. Within four days, the BEF had advanced

over 15 miles (24km), but their pace suddenly began to slow. Once again the defenders were able to move laterally more quickly than the attackers could move forward, the same problem the Germans had faced in the spring. At this point, Haig chose to halt the offensive, unlike Ludendorff before him, who had pressed his troops to breaking point. The rules of World War I dictated that there would be no breakthrough, and Haig had learned his lesson. Instead British forces attacked a week later further north, forcing the Germans to react by shifting their dwindling reinforcements in that direction. Once that attack had run its predictable course, it was abandoned, leading to a French attack further south and another German reaction.

The Allies had stumbled onto the operational level of warfare. A tactical victory in a single battle would not lead to a strategic victory in the war. However, a series of related tactical victories – ripping off great chunks of the German defensive network and forcing continued German troop movements – could lead to a strategic victory. In the '100 Days' battles of 1918 each tactical victory led logically to the next tactical victory, forcing the Germans further and further back towards their border and even breaching the vaunted Hindenburg Line in a matter of days.

Battered by continuing military defeat and haunted by famine and revolution at home, on 11 November 1918 the Germans quit World War I. Their defeat was not total, and the deeply flawed Treaty of Versailles would help to assure that the Great War was but the first total war for European and world dominance.

The Great War, far from being a tactical wasteland, had seen the military systems of the world change from lumbering linear forces into the deadly modern forces that would so devastate the globe in the next conflict. In a four-year period of innovation, modern warfare had been born. Commanders now presided over technological, professional forces. Weaponry had been altered for ever by

science, making war more efficient and more deadly. Many now saw armies as systems, vulnerable to deep penetrations. Others began to concentrate on the newly discovered operational level of war. Modern, industrialized nations seemed nearly impervious to decisive battlefield defeats. Only a series of coordinated battlefield efforts would suffice to win victory in a total war.

The new weapons, tactics and operational discoveries of the Great War would be the subject of many debates during the interwar period, especially among the vanquished. The victors, who had done so much to revolutionize warfare, would ignore the lessons of the Great War at their peril.

ABOVE: British Mark V heavy tanks of the 8th Tank Battalion move forward in the Battle of the St Quentin Canal. At this stage, tanks were seen primarily as infantry support weapons. Three of the tanks carry fascines, bundles of sticks used to help in crossing enemy trenches.

LEFT: In the US Army's first offensive of the Great War, American troops rush forward in order to launch an attack on the trenches of the veteran German Eighteenth Army at Cantigny. The soldier at bottom centre carries an example of the terrifying flamethrower; new weaponry and tactics had changed the very nature of infantry combat.

CHAPTER TWO

NEW THINKING

The interwar period saw many experiments in strategy and tactics. Among the most far-reaching were those involving mechanization and armour, both of which would impact on the role of the infantryman.

The nature of trench warfare during World War I led to high casualties each time armies clashed on the battlefield. For example, the 1916 Battle of Verdun, which lasted nearly 10 months, resulted in almost 800,000 casualties. On 1 July 1916, the first day of the Battle of the Somme, British casualties numbered over 57,000. By the time the battle ended six months later, the British had suffered 420,000 casualties, while the French lost 195,000 men and the Germans 650,000. The combined losses totalled over one million soldiers. When the war ended, the total casualties – killed, wounded, prisoners and missing – for the four-year conflict exceeded 37 million. While the Allied Powers suffered over 22 million casualties, the Central Powers lost over 15 million troops. These losses would have a huge impact on both the peace process and the nature of the military establishments in 1939 when war broke out again.

On 11 November 1918, an armistice ended the Great War. Following the cessation of hostilities, the leaders of the participating countries met at Versailles to negotiate a peace treaty. President Woodrow Wilson of the United States, Prime Minister David Lloyd George of Great Britain, Premier Georges Clemenceau of France,

LEFT: Technology revolutionized tactics and strategies between the wars. These Guardsmen, training at Pirbright, England, would become part of the reorganized British Army, which was the first to transform infantry units into machine-gun and rifle battalions, and mount them in motor vehicles.

ABOVE: A key to the new tactics was mobility. The British Army tested an all-mechanized force in the 1920s, and by the 1930s, reconnaissance units, like this detachment from the Northumberland Fusiliers, had finally traded in horses for motor vehicles.

and Prime Minister Vittorio Orlando of Italy tried to solve the world's problems at the Versailles Peace Conference, and they hoped that their solution would prevent future wars. At the same time, military leaders began to analyze the previous four years in order to develop new tactics designed to prevent the atrocities of trench warfare from being repeated in future conflicts.

Not all officers were ready to accept change, however. No one wanted a repeat of the horrific losses of the previous four years. Many political leaders and ordinary civilians thought that the solution lay in abolishing war; military leaders looked for a new weapon that would allow the quick defeat of an enemy. Some looked to the development of air power and strategic bombing, and others looked to the formation of tank divisions to reduce casualties, but most did not think that the infantry would become obsolete. Rather the infantry would play a secondary role to the air force or the tanks.

Although the military doctrines and organizations of the major powers

evolved between the world wars, a number of factors hindered the evolution of new weapons and tactics. A spirit of pacifism permeated the interwar period. The citizens of many nations rejected war and everything associated with the military. In addition, many nations felt the need to formalize their condemnation of war. Consequently, 15 countries signed the Kellogg–Briand Pact in 1928. A further 45 nations would add their names to the agreement, which stated that war was acceptable only for the self-defence of a nation.

Furthermore, governments, bowing to pressure both from their own citizens and from abroad, became increasingly reluctant to allocate funds for military research. A series of international conferences took place in the 1920s and 1930s. The purpose of these was to restrict the armaments of the militaries and navies of the major powers. Although not entirely successful, the delegates at the Washington Naval Conference negotiated restrictions on the number of capital ships that the participating countries could maintain. Some countries, such as the United States, downsized their armies by choice; others, like Germany, reduced the size of their armies because of the terms of the Versailles Peace Treaty.

ECONOMIC CONSTRAINTS

The United States and other countries could not justify the allocation of funds to develop new weapons when they had stockpiles of weapons and ammunition left over from World War I. By the time armies had depleted the stockpiles or could no longer use ammunition from the war, economic constraints impeded the production of new ones. While some governments were willing to finance the development and testing of new tactics and weapons, the Great Depression severely limited the availability of funds for tanks, aircraft, and other new equipment. Despite these limitations the mechanization of industry as well as the technological advances of the 1920s and 1930s would affect the conduct of the next war.

During the interwar period, the implementation of mass-production techniques increased industrial output and reduced costs. At the same time, the exploitation of raw materials, the construction of refineries and power plants, and agricultural productivity also grew. Scientific experimentation resulted in improvements in aviation, vehicles and communication. Better vehicles meant better cross-country transport abilities, the increased protection, firepower and speed of tanks and other armoured fighting vehicles, and the possibility of the rapid transportation of troops by means other than rail. All of these improvements would affect the nature of the next conflict.

There was, however, a downside to the rapid changes in technology. Concerned that the speed of these changes would quickly render them outdated, governments hesitated to invest in existing designs. In addition, officials had no way of predicting the effect of these technological advances on military tactics. Financial constraints frequently prevented the testing of new equipment before it was placed in the field. While many of the changes suggested the development of mechanized warfare, the leading military authorities did not always concur with this theory. The proponents of traditional combat arms resisted the push for tactical changes. The evolution of military tactics and weaponry proceeded at a different pace in each country.

By the end of World War I, the participating armies had undergone great changes. None of them were the same as they had been at the beginning of the conflict. By 1918 the most professional force in the field was the British Army, whose officers had been the first to understand the importance of operational thinking and the development of armoured equipment and doctrine. While other military officials had a narrow view of the uses of tanks in the field, British commanders took the lead in testing expanded roles for mechanized formations. Several British officers developed combined-arms tactics, beginning in 1918. Unlike his colleagues, however, Colonel J. F. C. Fuller placed much more emphasis on the role of tanks operating alone, rather than in conjunction with the infantry. In his Plan 1919, Fuller, drawing on German tactics, designed a large-scale armoured offensive, supported by air attacks against supply lines, that would result in a series of breakthroughs followed by the disruption of the enemy's headquarters. Once the enemy's command structure had been disrupted, British forces would launch follow-up attacks against the German front line. Unfortunately for Fuller, the war ended before he could convince his superiors to implement his plan.

BELOW: British experiments in mechanization proved the value of motor vehicles, and the United Kingdom was the first major power whose army switched completely from horse-drawn transport to internal combustion power. These British infantrymen pass in review, mounted in tracked personnel carriers developed from Carden-Loyd tankettes.

ABOVE: By the outbreak of World War II, troops like these members of the Royal Scots Fusiliers were entirely familiar with motor vehicles, part of their training being practice in rapid mounting and dismounting.

RIGHT: Fearful of another German invasion, successive French governments focused on improving their fixed defences. They built the Maginot Line, a massive chain of border fortifications, in which a large part of the strength of the French Army was garrisoned.

emphasis after the war was on the protection of the British Empire, few government officials supported Fuller's expensive plan. In addition, the tank programme, like those of the Royal Navy and the Royal Air Force, suffered from defence-spending cuts during the depression. Resistance to innovation impeded the tactical development of the British Army during the interwar period.

Because of their experiences with trench warfare, British commanders were determined to develop tactics that would return manoeuvrability to the battlefield. Consequently, they recognized the importance of mechanization. The establishment of the Royal Tank Corps in 1923 reflected the desire for change in order to build on the tank successes of World War I. In 1927 the British Army formed the Experimental Mechanical Force (EMF), which was one of the first all-arms mechanized formations, consisting of light and medium tanks and motorized machine-gunners, artillery and engineers. The EMF conducted brigade-level exercises that year and again the following year. In 1928, however, responding to opposition within the military community and budgetary problems, the British War Office disbanded the EMF.

British Army officers continued to debate the role of tanks in future

Although both the Germans and the Soviets studied them, Fuller's ideas did not gain wide acceptance in Great Britain. Conventional infantry commanders, although willing to utilize tank and air support, resisted the relegation of their troops to a minor role in future operations. Because the main

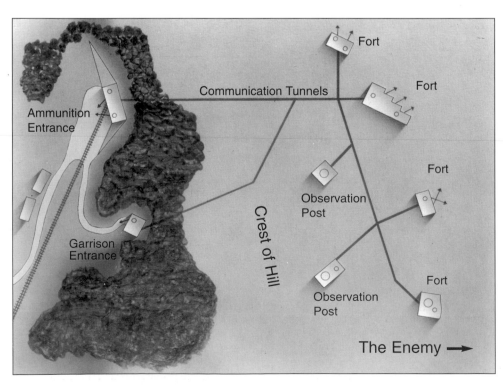

Fort
Fort
Communication Tunnels
Ammunition Entrance
Fort
Garrison Entrance
Crest of Hill
Observation Post
Fort
Observation Post
Fort
The Enemy →

conflicts. Although the EMF had been dissolved, its exercises in 1927 and 1928 had demonstrated the problem that resulted from the formation of a unit consisting of various types of motorized vehicles. Because some vehicles had tracks and others had wheels, they could only advance as a unit at slow speeds, which limited the EMF's ability to move rapidly. As a result, tank proponents began to accept one of Fuller's proposals: the creation of pure-tank units. The Royal Tank Corps began to press for the development of new tanks and new tank tactics.

The British military community did acknowledge, however, that the creation of tank formations would not eliminate the need for infantry units. A tank revolutionary, Percy Hobart, whose floating tanks landed on the Normandy beaches in 1944, advocated a primary role for tanks in future operations. Not all tank advocates went as far as Fuller and Hobart. George Lindsay, like those who supported more moderate change, suggested that tanks participate in combined-arms formations with support from mechanized infantry, artillery and other service. Some senior British military officials endorsed the use of tanks only as infantry support, while others, stressing their vulnerability, objected to the creation of independent armoured units. Despite their First World War experiences, die-hard cavalry supporters did not believe that tanks would replace horses on the battlefield.

As the debate continued within the British Army, another armour theorist,

Basil Liddell Hart, began to voice his opinion. An infantry officer during the Great War, Liddell Hart was influenced by Fuller's writings. He left the army in 1925 and pursued a career as a military correspondent, which enabled him to exert influence over the British Government in military matters. Unlike Fuller, however, Liddell Hart advocated a combined-arms force, with a large role for mechanized infantry; but he did not reject all of the theorist's ideas. In fact, he went beyond them. Liddell Hart expanded Fuller's proposal to use tanks in order to break through enemy lines. He envisaged the use of tanks to exploit the breakthrough and to advance deep behind enemy lines in order to disrupt its command centre.

PROPHETS WITHOUT HONOUR?

Although their ideas influenced the British Army, cuts in defence-spending by the late 1920s and 1930s, as well as the push for empire defence and the rejection of future continental conflicts, caused both Fuller and Liddell Hart to reconsider their positions. While Fuller began to focus more on strategic bombing, and less on tanks, to play the major role in future conflicts, Liddell Hart began to question whether or not armoured warfare could succeed against strong, well-prepared fortifications. Despite his uncertainty, Liddell Hart continued to influence those in power throughout the 1930s because of his position as private military adviser to Leslie Hore-Belisha, Secretary of State for War in the Chamberlain government.

LEFT: French soldiers in one of the Maginot Line's underground complexes in 1939. Unfortunately for French planners, in May 1940 the Germans declined to make a frontal assault on the line. Sweeping through Belgium and around the end of the defences, they isolated more than 400,000 French troops in their massively expensive but useless fortifications.

He argued against the deployment of troops on the Continent, advising that the government divert funds from ground troops to the improvement of the country's air defences. Liddell Hart's advice reflected growing concerns within the military community about the threat of strategic bombing.

The debate among infantry and tank commanders over the role of tanks did not prevent the formation of a division-sized independent mechanized force in 1934. Insufficient training, command disputes and other problems resulted in a poor showing by the force in its first armoured exercise. Following a change in command, the British mechanized a large percentage of its cavalry to create a Mobile Division in December 1937. The Mobile Division included two armoured cavalry brigades consisting of light tanks and armoured cars, one previously established tank brigade, two mechanized infantry battalions, and artillery, engineer and support formations. Although not fully equipped, the Mobile Division contained 500, mostly light, tanks. Without adequate guidance from their superiors, however, the cavalry officers in charge of the division decided to use it in the same way that they would use a cavalry division: for reconnaissance, screening and security. Within two years, the newly reorganized Mobile Division became the 1st Armoured Division.

Although the British developed tanks and combined-arms tactics, they failed to commence a study of World War I's lessons until 1932. The Army created a committee, which issued a report of its findings, but the chief of the imperial general staff did not allow it to circulate within the Army. In the late 1920s and 1930s the British Army implemented a series of experiments in order to analyze the potential of armoured warfare. These demonstrated the capability of tanks, as well as their limitations. As they developed tank and infantry tactics to be used in the next conflict, the British failed to incorporate the lessons from these experiments or those that they should have learned from the previous war. They did, however, restore the infantry's firepower and mobility with new equipment and organization, but the improvements imposed a cost. The British infantry battalion, although more mobile, had less firepower and limited antitank capabilities. By 1939, even though the British Army had developed new equipment and technology, it failed to devise tactics for using them effectively in the field. With the exception of the infantry battalion, combat arms and different weapons systems cooperation had improved little over what it had been in 1914.

FRENCH DEVELOPMENTS

During the 1920s and 1930s, while the British Army struggled to change despite economic, government and public constraints, the French faced different problems. According to the terms of the Versailles Treaty, Germany could maintain a 100,000-man professional army. As long as a German Army existed, France could not trust its former enemy, nor could it feel safe. Consequently, the French Army not only had to prepare for future conflicts, but also had to develop strong defensive capabilities to thwart an unexpected invasion. During the interwar period, although the French had a large army, it had little hope of deterring a sudden German attack because it consisted mainly of insufficiently trained reservists. France, like many other countries, did not want to invest in revitalizing its weary army, but believed that a German threat still existed. It was not a question of if Germany would attack again, but when. The French therefore allocated time and resources to the construction of a series of self-contained armed concrete forts: the Maginot Line. Recognizing how long it would take to mobilize their

BELOW: Japanese expansionism on the mainland of Asia meant that her troops saw combat a number of times during the 1930s. Here, gas-masked Japanese Marines fight through the rubble caused by the Imperial Air Force's bombardment of Shanghai, after the outbreak of war with China in 1937.

LEFT: The Soviets were among the pioneers of airborne operations. The Red Army was the first to deliver battalion and regimental-sized formations of infantry from the air, dropping paratroopers from TB-3 aircraft in military exercises through the 1930s. Ignored by most western armies, the exercises were avidly studied by the Germans.

reservists, French officers hoped to force the Germans to attack through Belgium, which would then give the army more time to prepare.

Feeling a sense of responsibility for their ally, French military strategists expected to come to Belgium's aid in the future; they therefore planned to fight the next war in Belgium, not at home. Unfortunately, Belgium's declaration of neutrality in 1936 prevented both the French and the British from deploying troops before the Germans invaded. Therefore, the French, in conjunction with the British, drew up plans for the rapid deployment of forces into Belgium and the Netherlands in the event of a German invasion. The French, responding to an emphasis by the military on mobility, allocated funds for the development of armoured forces. Because they considered them armoured infantry, the French commanders deployed their tanks throughout the army rather than in large independent formations. As a result, the role of tanks would be restricted initially to close infantry support. Because of their subordination to the infantry, the tanks' rate of advance was tied to the infantry.

By the early 1930s Maxime Weygand, the Chief of Staff, pushed for motorization and mechanization, despite limited funding. What with the Depression and the cost of constructing the Maginot Line, the military in general suffered from funding cuts. Because of

Weygand's fervent commitment to modernization, however, the military motorized seven infantry divisions and provided half-tracks and armoured cars for several cavalry divisions. In 1934 Weygand ordered the formation of the first light mechanized division, the *Division Légère Mécanique* (DLM). By the late 1930s, the French had established four DLMs. Because of his background as a cavalryman, Weygand assigned reconnaissance and security missions to the DLMs, rather than battlefield tasks.

In 1934 Lieutenant Charles de Gaulle's writings almost sabotaged the French Army's move toward modernization: he

ABOVE: Japanese control of Manchuria brought them into contact with the USSR. In 1938 and 1939, border disputes grew into wars in all but name, in which the Soviets had rather the better of things. These Japanese troops in Manchuria are about 50km (31 miles) from the combat zone on the Khalkin Gol river.

advocated the creation of an independent tank brigade that would advance in linear formation. A motorized infantry unit would follow the tank brigade for the purposes of mopping up. At a time when French citizens were promoting peace and the idea of citizen soldiers, de Gaulle proposed a large professional standing army that many feared could be used to start a war with Germany. Not willing to accept the slow modernization of the French Army, de Gaulle pushed for the rapid development of armour and tactics. The resulting debate contributed to the lack of French preparation for 1940. Although they had almost as many tanks as the Germans by 1940, the French did not establish their first armoured divisions until after war erupted. At that time the French Army consisted of a large, untrained, poorly organized militia and a small mechanized force. It was not until March 1940 that the French issued a regulation for large armoured-unit tactics. A few weeks later, German troops invaded France.

While pacifism entered the public debate in Great Britain and France, the Bolsheviks in the Soviet Union commenced preparations for armed conflict almost as soon as they came to power. Because of the ideological differences between Communism and capitalism, they believed that war was inevitable. Only total mobilization of their resources would result in a victory for the Soviets.

Despite the willingness to prepare, the actuality was somewhat different. In the 1920s the Soviets slowly developed their military capabilities. Following the industrial expansion plan of 1929, the armed forces, which grew in size, experienced rapid increases in the production of tanks and aircraft.

By 1928 Soviet military leaders had developed the 'Deep Battle' doctrine. According to Soviet military philosophy, a series of connected operational successes would lead ultimately to strategic victory. Despite the development of a doctrine, Soviet leaders did not agree on the nature of the future Red Army. An armour advocate, Mikhail N. Tukhachevsky, persuaded his superiors to create the army's first armoured divisions in 1931. Tukhachevsky, the guiding force behind the 'Deep Battle' doctrine, envisaged the deployment of conventional infantry and cavalry divisions, mechanized formations and aircraft, all working together to achieve the same goal: victory. According to Tukhachevsky's plan, the infantry working in concert with the other arms and weapons systems would launch a two-part battle. In the first phase, a massed force led by tanks would attack the enemy's front line on a narrow front and achieve a breakthrough of his conventional defences. Soviet artillery and mortars would silence the enemy's artillery and antitank guns. During the second phase, the rate of the tanks' advance would not be tied to that of the infantry. The tanks could exploit the hole in the enemy line to advance and scatter his reserves by launching small, deep attacks. The mobile elements of the force would move quickly in order to outflank the enemy or in order to penetrate the enemy's rear areas. Long-range artillery fire, bombing, parachute attacks, smoke and deception operations would support the main operation.

ARMOUR OR CONSCRIPTS

Despite the new doctrine, there was some opposition within the Soviet military leadership to devoting resources to the development of mechanized units at the expense of the infantry. Many still supported the concept of a large conscript army. As a result, the Soviets attempted to accomplish both the maintenance of a large conscript army and the development of a large armoured force.

Josef Stalin dealt the Soviet military a heavy blow in 1937 when he unleashed his secret police against his enemies. Most of the proponents of modernization, including Tukhachevsky, died during this purge. By 1939 the state had begun to dismantle the armoured division, and at a time when German panzer divisions were achieving their first successes.

In the United States, however, pacifism and the desire for isolation had an impact on the evolution of the military during the interwar period. Although some occupation troops remained in Austria until 1919 and in Germany until early 1923, most American servicemen quickly returned to the US and their families. The government authorized the reduction of America's armed forces. In 1920 Congress passed the National Defence Act which, had it been implemented, would have established the framework for the post-war army. In

the 1920s the US military, like that in Great Britain, suffered from budget cuts. After the Depression hit in 1929, military spending declined even more. Despite the reduction in funding, US military commanders, like their European counterparts, strove to improve their armed forces.

The United States Army, when it entered the field in 1918, had a unique organization. The infantry had a square division structure. By 1920, a number of American officers, including Generals Fox Conner and John Pershing, recommended the structural reorganization of infantry divisions. Copying the European triangular divisions, Pershing suggested the streamlining of the divisions and the development of new tactics. The majority of Pershing's proposals became the victims of infighting with his colleagues in the War Department; therefore, the structure of the square division remained virtually unchanged throughout the 1920s. Although an emphasis on officer training returned to mobile warfare in the mid-1920s, major alteration of equipment and organization did not occur until the mid-1930s because of budget cuts and the overall neglect of the army.

BELOW: Defeated armies often learn more from a battle than the victors, and by the time Hitler came to power in Germany, the new German Army was ready to revolutionize warfare. Based on their infiltration tactics of 1918, to which was added mobile armour and motorization of the infantry, their new idea of warfare was called *Blitzkrieg*.

SHORTSIGHTED AMERICANS

While the US Army focused on the infantry, it neglected the development of mechanized and armoured forces. The subordination of the tank forces to the infantry resulted in a plan to use the tanks as support for the infantry in breakthrough attacks. By the end of the 1920s, British experiments with mechanized forces began to have an impact on the US Army, which conducted its own tests with Experimental Armoured Forces (EAF) in 1928 and 1929. Although a permanent force was created the following year, the Depression caused budget cuts that forced its elimination. Chief of Staff Douglas MacArthur (1930–35) continued to push for army-wide mechanization and motorization, but the budgetary problems forced him to limit his mechanized experiments to the cavalry units.

In 1935 the situation began to change when General Malin Craig, who agreed with the reforms advocated by Conner and others, became the US Army's Chief of Staff. Craig immediately ordered a General Staff board to reassess the army's combat organization and tactics. He also suggested that the board consider the formation of small, mobile divisions that could use mechanical rather than human power. In its report the board suggested that the divisions be reorganized along the lines used by European armies. On numerous occasions between 1936 and 1939, the 2nd Infantry Division tested

RIGHT: The Germans, like the Soviets, tested many of their weapons as well as their tactics during the Spanish Civil War. Here a Messerschmitt Bf 109 strafes Republican troops during the Battle of Madrid.

BELOW: Disliked by many in the German Army, Hitler's SS bodyguard, the *Leibstandarte Adolf Hitler*, was organized as a motorized regiment. Its first major operation was the occupation of Austria after the *Anschluss*.

the new formation. In 1939 General George Marshall became the chief of staff. Like his predecessors, he was committed to mechanization and the development of new tactics. Consequently, he ordered the army to conduct a series of exercises to test combined-arms operations. The Third Army conducted the first large-scale GHQ manoeuvres in 1940.

LESSONS FROM DEFEAT

In some ways, defeat surprised Germany in 1918. As soon as the war ended, the military launched an investigation to determine what had happened. While the victors for the most part had no compelling reason to race towards change, the Germans welcomed new weapons and tactics with open arms. General Hans von Seeckt played a key role in the evolution of the German Army during the interwar period.

In addition to his job of rebuilding the defeated army, based on his own experiences on the Russian Front, Seeckt concluded that an immobile mass army could be outmanoeuvred by a smaller, highly trained, mobile force. Mobility and surprise would take precedence over firepower. The German commanders studied the writings of Fuller and Liddell Hart. Once Seeckt and his staff had devised a doctrine, they ordered the appropriate organization and equipment. Industries designed technological developments in order to achieve the doctrine.

From the start, Seeckt circumvented the terms of the Versailles Treaty. Forced to reduce the officer corps, he selected the best general staff officers and ordered them to rebuild the military. In addition, he created the basis for Germany's early successes in the next war. In order to do this, Seeckt incorporated traditional German military tactics: a concentrated force on a narrow front to achieve a breakthrough, and the integration of weapons and arms in order to overcome the defences of the enemy.

He also emphasized a decentralized command structure that allowed the commanders to make their own tactical decisions. Although some German commanders disagreed with him, Seeckt stressed the importance of modernization and of tanks. Despite the

restrictions imposed by the Treaty of Versailles, German officers designed an armoured doctrine and secretly tested tanks in the Soviet Union.

When developing the new doctrine, the German commanders had to consider the nature of the next war. Numerous officers believed that tanks should be used only as infantry support; others believed that antitank guns would make tanks far too vulnerable in the field. After Hitler came to power, the armoured theorists gained more and more support, and generally succeeded in implementing some of their best and most ingenious ideas.

One of the most influential supporters of mechanization was Heinz Guderian. Guderian advocated the establishment of new all-arms mechanized formations that would magnify the effectiveness of the tank and facilitate mobile warfare. With Hitler's support, the German General Staff began to execute a new mechanization policy. Various antitank units, engineer companies and infantry divisions received orders to become motorized.

The new German doctrine extended beyond mechanization and tanks to the development of close air support for ground operations. Although ultimately committed to strategic bombing and the concept of air power, the Luftwaffe commanders agreed to allocate resources for ground support. With the integration of air and mechanized formations into ground operations, the Germans moved closer to the development of the famous 'Blitzkrieg', or lightning warfare, tactics. These new tactics would be unleashed for the first time in Poland on 1 September 1939.

ABOVE: Germany's secret plans to re-arm came out into the open in 1935, when Hitler cast aside the shackles of Versailles. Plans to re-equip the *Wehrmacht* were under way, but for the moment the General Staff had to use dummy tanks made from plywood and canvas to try out their new theories of mobile war.

CHAPTER THREE

BLITZKRIEG

The German campaigns of 1939 and 1940 introduced the world to a new word and a new kind of battle: *Blitzkrieg* or 'Lightning war.' Using new tactics, the Wehrmacht swept triumphantly through Europe.

The nature of World War II not only forced armies to incorporate all available weapons and arms into mobile, flexible units, but it also made them adapt to numerous threats, terrain and climates. Several trends emerged during the course of the war.

First, mechanized combined-arms forces matured during this period. Although most armies in 1939 considered armoured divisions as a limited, supported mass of tanks, by 1943 armoured divisions had evolved to become a balance of various combat arms and support services. Second, due to the concentration of mechanized forces into mobile divisions, ordinary infantry units lacked the necessary defensive antitank weapons, as well as armoured vehicles, for the offensive. Third, the desire to thwart *Blitzkrieg* drove these trends. Fourth, both the environments and the fluid tactics of the war fostered the creation of specialized combat units, such as amphibious and airborne divisions. Fifth, a war conducted strictly with ground operations ended with World War II. Finally, major changes in command, control, communications and intelligence resulted from the emergence of the complicated, multidimensional conflicts of this war.

LEFT: Spearheading Germany's invasion of France in May 1940, a Panzer IV of the Wehrmacht bursts through the Ardennes Forest. Rapidly advancing toward the Channel coast, the tanks and their accompanying infantry and artillery demonstrated the main characteristic of a successful *Blitzkrieg*: speed.

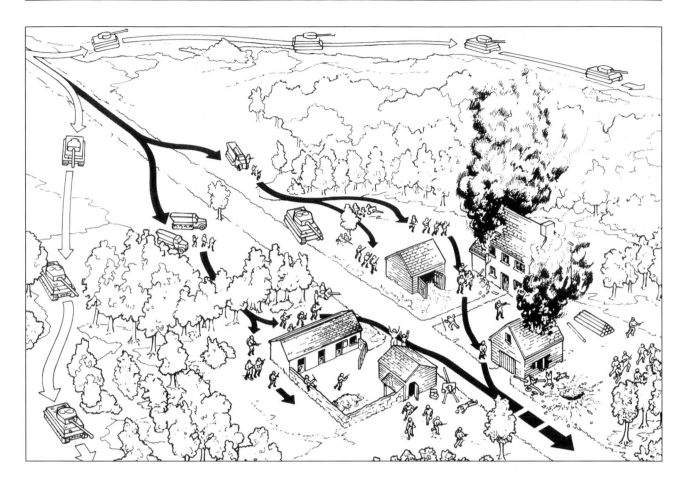

Although not completely developed until the inter-war period, *Blitzkrieg* tactics can be traced back to the German spring offensive of 1918. The Germans, even though they did not use tanks, succeeded in disrupting and demoralizing their opponents. After the war, General Hans von Seeckt built upon the 1918 German tactics to develop 'Blitzkrieg', or lightning war. The new doctrine that resulted extended beyond mechanization and tanks to the development of close air support for ground operations. Mobility and surprise would take precedence over firepower. Under Seeckt's direction, the German military developed the capability of implementing offensive campaigns which were always fast-moving.

The *Blitzkrieg* doctrine stressed several important ideas. First, the situation on the battlefield had changed. Mechanization and technological advancements brought modern war. As a result, the situation dictated 'decentralized, mission-oriented orders'. Second, two factors would dominate the field: speed, and the exploitation of the enemy's weaknesses. Therefore, troop commanders, whether operating on the offensive or the defensive, had to adapt to the fluidity of the battle. They could not afford to wait for orders to come from their superior officers. Third, the various combat branches could no longer function alone. The new modern war required closer coordination and cooperation between them. Finally, unlike during the previous war, commanders could not lead from headquarters established well to the rear of the front lines. Because the new tactics were designed to exploit any given situation on the battlefield, the commanders had to be close enough to the front lines to issue appropriate orders. Using air-supported panzer divisions, the Germans hoped to overwhelm the enemy at a particular point and achieve a breakthrough, before finally advancing rapidly and then encircling the defenders.

While Seeckt and other commanders developed the new German military doctrine in the 1930s, Germany began to test the provisions of the Versailles Treaty under the leadership of Adolf Hitler. Despite limits imposed on the size of the

German Army by the treaty, Hitler ordered the implementation of massive rearmament. Between 1933 and 1939 the size of the army and armoured forces greatly increased. In March 1936 German troops occupied the demilitarized Rhineland, breaking another provision of the treaty. Two years later, Germany implemented the *Anschluss*, or union with Austria. Once Austria was controlled, Germany turned to another neighbour, Czechoslovakia. Using the mistreatment of Germans in the Sudetenland as an excuse, German forces moved toward the Czech border.

As tensions increased and Hitler refused to back down, Benito Mussolini suggested a conference in Munich to resolve the situation. Hitler agreed. On 24 September 1938 Hitler and Mussolini met with British Prime Minister Neville Chamberlain and French President Edouard Daladier. No government officials from the Soviet Union or Czechoslovakia received an invitation to participate in the proceedings in Munich. Bowing to pressure from Hitler and Mussolini, and armed with Hitler's assurance that he had no quarrel with the rest of Czechoslovakia, Chamberlain and Daladier agreed to allow German occupation and control of the Sudetenland. Chamberlain returned to Great Britain and announced that he and his colleagues had achieved peace. All could breathe a sigh of relief. The great leaders had averted war, but not for long.

SEIZURE OF CZECHOSLOVAKIA

Following the Munich Conference, the economic situation hindering German rearmament did not improve. What Germany needed was an influx of resources and industry. Control of the rest of Czechoslovakia would fulfil this need. Hitler just needed an excuse to occupy the neighbouring country. The Czechs provided one. In March 1939 a political crisis broke out. Hitler took advantage of the situation and ordered German forces to invade Czechoslovakia and seize the capital, Prague. The Germans hit the jackpot. After entering Czechoslovakia, German troops seized over 1200 aircraft, 800 tanks, almost 2000 antitank guns, 2300 field artillery pieces and 57,000 machine guns, and over 600,000 rifles. Although the Germans could celebrate the addition of these materials to their rearmament stash, their action in Czechoslovakia would bring unforeseen consequences.

BELOW: On 1 September 1939, German troops crossed the Polish frontier to launch the war in Europe. Here, a mixed column of cavalry and infantry move into the Polish corridor towards Danzig (now Gdansk).

A bitter outburst of public outrage in Great Britain forced Chamberlain to reconsidered his country's diplomatic position. Not ready to recognize that war was unavoidable, Neville Chamberlain implemented a diplomatic policy to prevent further German aggression in Europe. At the same time, he had to acknowledge that Britain's armed forces were unprepared should war erupt on the Continent. As a result, the British Government allocated funds for rearmament and admitted the importance of the army's role on the Continent. In addition, the British Government, realizing the possibility of Germany's next goal, guaranteed the independence of Poland. Hitler took two actions in response.

On 3 April 1939 he ordered the OKW (Oberkommando der Wehrmacht, or the Armed Forces High Command) to prepare for the invasion of Poland. The codename of the operation was Case White. In August 1939 the Führer announced that he and Stalin had signed the Nazi–Soviet Non-Aggression Pact, in which Germany and the Soviet Union put aside their differences for the time being in order to accomplish a common goal: the division of Poland. According to the Case White plan, two army groups, carrying out a war of manoeuvre and penetration, would attack and encircle the Polish forces. Commanded by

General Ludwig Beck, Army Group North, which included the Third and Fourth Armies, would advance into East Prussia before turning south and heading for Warsaw. Commanded by General Gerd von Rundstedt, Army Group South, consisting of the Eighth, Tenth and Fourteenth Armies, would advance through Silesia to occupy the Vistula on both sides of Warsaw. Encircling the Polish defenders, the two army groups would then systematically destroy them.

Forty infantry, six panzer, four light and four motorized divisions would carry out Case White. More than 1300 aircraft would supply air support for the offensive. Including 30 divisions, 11 cavalry brigades and two mechanized brigades, the Polish Army, with fewer than 900 tanks at its disposal, would be greatly outnumbered. Only one-third of the army's formations would be at full strength when the German offensive began. The Polish Army also lagged behind the German Army in terms of artillery, mobility and communications. Because they were so badly outnumbered, the Poles had to weaken their defences in their industrial regions in order to station more forces to areas on the border with Germany.

Having set an initial target date of 26 August, the Germans began mobilization on 15 August. Last-ditch efforts to find a peaceful resolution to the tensions on the

RIGHT: As German columns sliced through Poland in two giant pincers, Polish resistance began to collapse. Himmler's armed SS received its baptism of fire during the campaign: here the *Leibstandarte* have attacked enemy forces near Sacharzow.

Polish border resulted in a delay. On 31 August, however, Hitler issued Directive No. 1, ordering the commencement of Case White the next day.

On 1 September 1939 the Nazis unleashed *Blitzkrieg* against Poland. While the Luftwaffe attacked Polish air bases and military targets in Warsaw, German tanks and infantrymen rammed into the defenders. In less than three weeks, German forces occupied over half of the country. German aircraft bombed and strafed the enemy soldiers and overwhelmed Polish aircraft in the air. By 4 September, the Luftwaffe controlled the skies over Poland and could devote its full strength to supporting the ground offensive and to attacking the enemy's railway system. Attacks by the Luftwaffe caused the collapse of the Polish forces concentrating in the region west of Warsaw. As German aircraft disrupted the enemy defenders, Army Group North burst through the Polish Corridor between East Prussia and Pomerania, and Army Group South proceeded to push towards Lodz and Kraków.

COLLAPSE OF POLAND

Under the weight of German attacks, Polish resistance collapsed within a week. On 7 September the Polish High Command withdrew from Warsaw, which caused it to lose control of its forces. Polish resistance forced the advancing Germans to implement a second pincer movement in the area east of the Vistula toward the River Bug. By 16 September the German forces had trapped the defending formations between the Rivers Vistula and Bug. German ground and air forces prepared to demolish the encircled Poles. On 16 September German aircraft dropped more than 700,000 bombs on the trapped enemy. Two days later 120,000 Polish soldiers – one-fourth of the Polish Army – surrendered to the Germans.

Although 100,000 Polish soldiers continued to defend Warsaw, the Germans were close to a decisive victory. Under the threat of massive destruction to the defending troops – as well as to the civilian population – from German air and artillery bombardments, the soldiers in Warsaw decided to surrender. As the Germans thrashed the Polish forces in the west, Soviet troops entered into the conflict from the east. Claiming their desire to 'protect' the population as a motive, Soviet forces advanced into Poland on 17 September.

By the end of the month, Polish resistance had virtually ended. The last surrender of Polish troops occurred on 6 October 1939. The total Polish casualties numbered over 900,000 – 70,000 killed, 133,000 wounded and 700,000 captured. The Germans, on the other hand, suffered fewer than 45,000 total casualties: 11,000 were killed, 30,000 wounded, and 3400 missing.

ABOVE: France and Britain declared war on Germany following the invasion of Poland, but did little more than bring their defences to a high state of alert. Here, French soldiers, seen on 27 October 1939, man an artillery observation post somewhere on the Maginot Line at the German border.

ABOVE: German infantry crosses the River Meuse. They established a bridgehead on the other side, allowing the Panzers to cross within hours. Allied planners had expected that it would take the Germans four days.

the OKH opposed Manstein's plan as too risky, Rundstedt supported it. Hitler approved the plan in March.

On 10 May 1940 the Germans unleashed Case Yellow. It began with air attacks. Using its advantage in numbers of modern aircraft, the Luftwaffe planned to achieve air superiority. To accomplish this objective, German air forces attacked Allied air bases and targeted bridges spanning the rivers Lek, Waal and Maas. As a result, the Luftwaffe divided the Netherlands in two and totally disrupted the enemy's defences. The Luftwaffe suffered heavy losses during the first few days of the battle, but it accomplished two goals: German aircraft gained air superiority, and provided support for the effort on the ground. As the Luftwaffe attacked the Netherlands, German paratroopers gained control of the major bridges leading into Holland. Once they held the bridges, the 9th Panzer Division burst through the enemy's defences and advanced into the country. Four days later, the Dutch surrendered.

With the Luftwaffe providing cover, German panzer and infantry divisions continued the march to the west. As Army Group B rolled into Belgium, French and British forces raced to stop

would attack the Low Countries. After defeating the Dutch and the Belgians, the group would tie down the French and British troops that rushed to the defence of Belgium and prevent them from advancing to stop Army Group A. Army Group C would implement a deceptive attack against the Maginot Line to prevent French formations from moving to the Ardennes Forest. Although

the advancing Germans. German glider troops attacked and captured Eben Emael, the Belgian fortress situated at the juncture of the Albert Canal and the River Meuse. After the fortress fell, Army Group B's infantry divisions swiftly marched into the centre of the country. The Belgian Army did not recover from the initial blows launched by the enemy. Convinced that they had been right and that the Germans planned to advance through Belgium and attack France, the French High Command ordered more French and British troops to the country in order to stop the enemy.

ARDENNES SURPRISE

While the French and British focused on Belgium, Army Group A launched the main German attack through the Ardennes Forest. Spearheaded by Panzer Group Kleist, which was protected by air cover, Army Group A easily cracked the weak French defences. Their advance through the forest caught the enemy off guard and proceeded so smoothly that by the evening of 12 May seven panzer divisions, followed by infantry and motorized units, neared the River Meuse. The next day the Germans opened a furious attack against the French defenders. The 7th Panzer Division's infantry, commanded by General Erwin Rommel, crossed the river, drove the enemy back and quickly constructed a bridge across the Meuse. German panzers raced across the bridge and established a bridgehead. Allied forces reached the river too late to stop the German advance; fleeing refugees clogged the roads and impeded their progress. Panicking, some soldiers fled rather than engage the enemy in battle. By 14 May Guderian's 1st and 2nd Panzer Divisions crossed the river further south. Two days later, Army Group A turned north, and then raced towards the English Channel.

The rapid advance through the Ardennes Forest caught the OKW off guard. They had not finalized plans for the next phase of the operation. Despite the opposition of French forces, the spearheads of Panzer Group Kleist pushed them back and drove across open country on 19 May. On 20 May advance elements reached the Channel, with British and French troops retreating in

front of them. Germany infantrymen struggled to keep up with the panzer group, but they succeeded in securing the encirclement of the enemy forces. The French launched a weak counterattack from the south on 19 May, while the British attacked from the north on 21 May. But these counterattacks had little effect on the advancing enemy. Neither the French nor the British had the reserves necessary to stop the Germans.

The situation got progressively worse as German forces moved up the coast. Misreading the situation, Hitler, who feared that the British and the French could mount an effective counterattack, ordered the panzers to stop on 24 May and consolidate their forces with the

BELOW: Italy's invasion of the Balkans quickly ran into trouble. In April 1941 Hitler was forced to commit forces to help the Italians, just when they were most needed in the build-up for the invasion of Russia. The spring thaw and muddy road conditions made rapid movement of forces difficult.

infantry. Bowing to pressure from the advancing enemy, the Belgian Army surrendered on 28 May. With the French First Army providing protection, the British Expeditionary Force (BEF) organized the evacuation of troops from Dunkirk: 'Operation Dynamo'. Although they had to abandon their heavy equipment and many of their weapons, most of the BEF avoided capture by the Germans. Between 31 May and 3 June, a total of approximately 340,000 Allied troops managed to escape.

On 5 June, Army Group B launched the final phase of their Western Europe campaign, *Fall Rot*, or Case Red. The French stiffly defended against the German onslaught. The 7th Panzer Division, led by Rommel, seized two railway bridges that spanned the River Somme. After crossing the Somme, the

OPPOSITE: Mussolini's grandiose plans for empire led him into military adventures for which the Italian Army was unprepared. Poorly equipped and poorly led, the Italians needed Hitler and the Wehrmacht to help them out in Yugoslavia, Greece, and North Africa.

division moved towards the River Seine. Within six weeks from the start of the offensive, over 98,000 French soldiers surrendered to the 7th Panzer Division, which also seized numerous guns, tanks and armoured vehicles. By 9 June, the Germans had pierced the French defences all along the front. Army Group A, pushing aside enemy troops, moved deeper into France. No longer willing to allow the destruction of the country, the French Government surrendered Paris on 14 June and signed an armistice on 22 June 1940. Three and a half million troops fell to the Germans, who only had 45,000 of their soldiers killed in the process. The Germans had again successfully implemented combined-arms tactics in order to achieve their goal. Panzer, infantry and aircraft formations had perfected the *Blitzkrieg* tactics which they had employed in Poland less than a year earlier.

The German victory in France seemed to validate *Blitzkrieg*. Unlike the earlier campaign in Poland, the Germans focused their mechanized forces in large groups in key locations along the front. Supported by five motorized divisions, seven panzer divisions moved through the Ardennes Forest along a 70-km (44-mile) front. British and French forces, on the other hand, were spread thinly along a wide front in a linear defensive position. The German thrust easily broke through a point of the enemy's linear defence. By 14 May German mobile

forces accomplished deep exploitation of the enemy. The French, thrown off guard by the rapid enemy advance, could not react quickly because of their command and control structure. The lack of enemy resistance in the rear enabled the German commanders to use armoured reconnaissance formations to lead their column's advance. The better organization of their armoured divisions gave the Germans another advantage over the British and the French. In addition, the division of the German panzer formation command structure into a series of subordinate headquarters enabled the commanders to operate effectively in the field. Combat engineers made road repairs, which facilitated the Germans' rapid advance over the poor roads of the Ardennes Forest. A coordinated supporting effort by tanks, artillery, and tactical aircraft enabled German infantry and engineers to cross the River Meuse on 13 May. The rapid defeat of France demonstrated the importance of a number of factors: combined-arms mechanized formations, penetration attacks, exploitation of the enemy's rear, and the Germans' advantage in combined-arms training as well as procedures.

Following the defeat of France, however, events did not progress as Hitler had hoped. On 10 June 1940, before the French collapse, Italy declared war on Britain and France. First, the next phase in the German strategy would fail. Then, before Hitler's forces could implement an offensive against another enemy – the Soviet Union – Italian expansionist military actions would force German troops to become involved in the Balkans and in North Africa.

BALKAN ADVENTURE

Jealous of the German acquisition of European territory, Mussolini decided that Italy was entitled to expand its holdings. By the summer of 1940, Mussolini looked to the Balkans as the solution to retrieving Italy's lost glory. Following a series of incidents, Greece refused to accept an ultimatum from Italy. Consequently, on 28 October, Italy attacked Greece; Britain promised Greece support. It did not take long for the Italian offensive to go horribly wrong. On 3 November, Greek forces

BELOW: Waffen SS troops of the *Leibstandarte Adolf Hitler* Division manhandle a motorbike across rough Greek terrain in May 1941. Although administratively separate from the army, in combat SS units were under the command of the Wehrmacht general staff.

captured 5000 Italian soldiers. Ignoring this setback, Italy invaded Albania five days later. As Italy's military position in the Balkans deteriorated, Hitler considered sending troops in to the rescue. Greek forces repeatedly stopped the Italian advances in Northern Greece and Albania. As they forced the Italians to retreat, the Greeks captured several important Albanian cities. Issuing Directive No 20 on 13 December, Hitler ordered preparation for 'Operation Marita': relief of the stalled Italian operation in Albania. At the end of the month, Mussolini appealed to Hitler for help in Albania. A month later, with Directive No 22 Hitler reiterated his intention to supply this. Despite the November and December directives, however, German forces did not enter the fray in the Balkans for several months. They did, though, become committed elsewhere in the Mediterranean region, particularly in North Africa.

YUGOSLAVIA ATTACKED

Following the overthrow of the Yugoslav Government on 25 March, Hitler signed Directive 25, which ordered German troops to destroy the country, and he authorized the bombing of Belgrade. The code name for the operation was 'Punishment'. On 6 April 1941 the Luftwaffe launched bombing missions against Belgrade and virtually destroyed the Yugoslav air force on the ground. While the Luftwaffe bombed the capital, German, Italian, and Hungarian forces invaded Yugoslavia from the north. German infantry quickly over-ran Yugoslavia. Leading the way, German troops quickly ruptured the Yugoslav defences. On 12 April, a day after Italian forces began to advance along the coast, Belgrade surrendered. Pressured by both the Italian and German armies, the Greek Army withdrew from Albania. The Germans occupied Sarajevo on 15 April. Two days later, Yugoslavia surrendered. The Germans seized a total of over 330,000 prisoners.

At the same time as they were gaining ground in Yugoslavia, German forces continued their offensive in Greece, the Wehrmacht's second Balkan operation. In many respects, the German campaign in Greece mirrored the one in

Yugoslavia. Attacking southwards along a wide front, XXXX Panzer Corps outflanked Greek defences and forced Greek and British troops to retreat before them. The Luftwaffe's overwhelming air superiority convinced the British to withdraw from Greece. By the end of April, the British had completed their evacuation, and the Germans and Italians occupied Greece.

After the subsequent fall of Crete, the Germans turned their attention to two other regions: North Africa and the Soviet Union. As had been the case in the Balkans, Italian military action in North Africa resulted in German military participation in the region. The Italians' first venture into colonial expansion had occurred before the outbreak of war in Europe. Between 1935 and 1936 they had conquered Ethiopia. By end of the decade, Mussolini was ready to restore the Roman Empire in the Mediterranean. Following the Italian declaration of war on Britain and France in June 1940, a series of raids began in North Africa, which escalated into a full-scale conflict.

In July 1940 Italian air forces attacked Alexandria while ground troops seized British outposts on the Sudanese border. Throughout the month, Italian forces continued to harass the British in Egypt. By early August, after concentrating on the Libya–Egypt border, Italian troops attacked British Somaliland. By the middle of the month, the Italians had forced British troops to vacate British

ABOVE: Egypt 1942. A large proportion of Rommel's *Afrika Korps* was actually provided by the Italian Army. In spite of their poor showing against the British in 1940 and 1941, the best Italian units performed well when following good leadership.

Somaliland. A few days later the Italian invasion of Egypt began. Following the capture of Sidi Barrani, 97km (60 miles) from the frontier, the Italians began to build their fortified camps.

The small British force stationed in the Middle East had received pre-war training to high standards, but it was poorly equipped. In mid-1940, however, Churchill ordered the transfer of what little resources Britain had to Egypt to counter the threat from Libya. Consequently, a single battalion of 48 heavily armoured infantry support tanks (Mark II or Matilda) travelled to Egypt. The battalion joined two understrength, but well-trained, British divisions. The British spent the next several months solving several logistical problems and also preparing to go on the offensive against the Italian forces.

On 9 December the British launched their attack. The 4th Indian Infantry Division, in conjunction with infantry support tanks, moved against the poorly supplied Italian infantry. The Italians had protected their camps with minefields and obstacles. Recognizing the dangers of a frontal assault, the British advanced between the Italian camps, attacked them from the west, and moved forward along the unmined entrance roads to each camp. While artillery and mortar fire distracted and pinned down the Italian defenders, two companies of infantry tanks, supported by platoons carrying Bren machine guns, attacked. After the tanks broke through the enemy's defences, trucks drove up, and infantrymen dismounted and proceeded to mop up the defeated Italians.

Advantages in superior training, mobility, and equipment resulted in the British victory in Egypt in December 1940. Following the Italian fiasco in Egypt, Mussolini appealed to Hitler for help. The introduction of German troops into the North African theatre would negate the British advantages there. In addition, because of obligations in other theatres, the British reduced the size of their forces in Egypt in early 1941 and early 1942. Consequently, the Germans were to face a partially trained and poorly equipped enemy when they attacked in March 1941.

In early February 1941 General Erwin Rommel arrived in North Africa to assume control of the German *Afrika Korps*. Because of the vast, open, desert spaces, the fight for North Africa would be characterized by the rapid movement of troops. Spearheaded by tank formations, motorized infantry quickly

BELOW: Not all of the fighting in North Africa occurred in open desert areas. Here, South African troops use grenades and gunfire while fighting their way through the ruined houses of Sollum, Libya.

advanced across the desert. Rommel had orders to protect Tripoli and the remaining Italian troops. Quickly assessing the situation, he realized that in order to succeed, he must go on the offensive. Led by armoured forces, the Germans attacked and disrupted the new, poorly acclimatized British troops. Rommel pushed the British nearly 644km (400 miles), and forced them out of Libya. They managed to hold only Tobruk. Lacking the power needed to destroy the enemy, though, Rommel's force remained between two British strongholds: Tobruk, and the defences along the Egyptian frontier.

BRITISH AMATEURISM

Despite their obligations in Europe and their new offensive in the Soviet Union, the Germans' fight for North Africa had not yet ended. The two British advantages – having broken the German code and possessing air superiority – did not, however, outweigh their weaknesses on the ground. Despite their superiority in numbers of tanks, the British had to divide their tanks between Tobruk and the Egyptian frontier. Due to the German victories and demands for counteroffensives by the British Government, British commanders in the desert had no time to analyze their mistakes and to correct them through additional training. In addition, the constant turnover in command prevented the British troops from learning the lessons of desert warfare. Furthermore, when newly trained formations arrived in Egypt, the British commanders frequently applied them in a piecemeal fashion, which reduced their effectiveness. Unlike the British commanders, who generally had not studied combined-arms tactics, the Germans arrived in North Africa with several tactical advantages: a system of combined-arms formations, flexible commanders, and tactics designed to utilize mass combat power.

When they arrived in North Africa, the Germans also had certain other advantages over the British. Because the British continued to use unsecured communications, the Germans easily intercepted their unencrypted messages. The Germans' medium tanks were better-armed and armoured than the

British light tanks. During the desert battles of 1941 and 1942, the lack of armoured vehicles or effective antitank guns increased the vulnerability of Commonwealth troops. Numerous British armoured units, because they considered the infantry a nuisance, returned to mindset of pure-armour cavalry. In June 1941, the British learned the folly of launching a tank attack without first identifying the location of the enemy's antitank gun line. Following the rapid loss of 17 tanks, the British recognized the importance of firepower over other battlefield elements. In addition, the tendency of armoured units to operate alone and leave infantry formations exposed increased the already growing mistrust and hindered combined-arms cooperation.

Confident, thanks to his numerous successes in North Africa, Rommel wanted to keep the British off balance. He advocated an advance into Egypt, and Hitler agreed. But neither Rommel nor Hitler realized the toll that the previous months had taken on the *Afrika Korps*, which would be unable to drive to Alexandria unless the British defences shattered. The culmination of the *Afrika Korps'* thrust into Egypt was the turning point of the North Africa campaign: the Battle of El Alamein, in July 1942.

ABOVE: As leader of the *Afrika Korps*, Erwin Rommel applied the theories of rapid movement and flexibility he had learned as an infantry officer on the Italian front in 1918 to tank warfare in North Africa. His initial successes made him a national hero in Germany. Following the German capture of Tobruk in June 1942, Hitler promoted Rommel to the rank of Field Marshal.

TOP: When reinforcing a defensive position, all weapons were utilized. Here, a dug-in British Cruiser tank turret was used as an antitank weapon.

ABOVE: Australian troops attack a German position at El Alamein. Commonwealth troops first stopped the overstretched *Afrika Korps* in midsummer, before taking the offensive under General Bernard L. Montgomery.

Before the battle, however, the British Eighth Army would receive a new commander, Field Marshal Bernard Montgomery, who had only three months in which to prepare for the next offensive. From the beginning, British commanders did not always succeed in using the correct tactics to counter the German combined-arms task organization concept. While still in England, Montgomery identified the weaknesses of the British approach in North Africa. The British tendency to form small combined-arms task forces affected the divisions' ability to operate effectively. The numerous small task forces frequently suffered defeat at the hands of the *Afrika Korps'* concentrated actions. Although some British commanders in Egypt made attempts to adapt the theory of combined-arms armoured divisions, the next German offensive began before the British units could execute the necessary organizational and tactical changes.

Following his arrival in North Africa, Montgomery initiated a retraining programme. Because he could not completely change the existing procedures, he looked for ways in which to adapt traditional command and control methods to desert warfare. When the British stopped the German advance at Alam Haifa in September 1942, they bought time to implement changes. Montgomery used the time to prepare the Eighth Army for the El Alamein offensive of October–November 1942. He returned to the combined-arms tactics of World War I, in which each corps controlled its own artillery. The first step of Montgomery's plan involved a night penetration of enemy defensive positions by engineers, infantry, and artillery. Protected by these forces, armoured units would advance and tempt the Germans to counterattack. Montgomery hoped to take advantage of the Eighth Army's strengths at a time when the enemy was experiencing fuel and equipment shortages that would impede their manoeuvrability. The result of Montgomery's strategy was a battle of attrition, in which the general frequently adapted his plans to suit the actuality of the battlefield in front of him.

THE TURN OF THE TIDE

In late August the Germans attacked the British position at El Alamein, but they were driven back. Instead of exploiting his success, however, Montgomery focused on preparations for the October campaign. According to his plan, his forces would mount several diversionary attacks to make the Germans turn to the south. Then the main thrust would hit the *Afrika Korps'* northern flank. Relying on artillery and engineers to cut a path through the Germans' mined defensive position, the British forces would pierce the enemy's defences and achieve a breakthrough. The offensive did not, however, proceed as planned.

On 23 October the offensive began with a heavy artillery barrage. After the barrage, the infantry attacked. But because the paths cleared through the minefields were too narrow, the infantry advance stalled, and the British armoured force became stuck in the open minefields. Fortunately for the British, Rommel was on sick leave in Germany, and he did not return until the battle had been raging for 48 hours. The German commanders failed to react quickly to the British assault. They committed their forces to the battle in a piecemeal

fashion. Yet although the 15th Panzer Division lost 75 per cent of its tanks on the first day, German resistance did not falter; in fact, it continued.

Realizing that his plan was not succeeding, Montgomery ordered his force to redeploy on 27 October. The next day the Germans took a heavy blow in the north. Although they failed to breach the enemy's defences, the British reduced Rommel's armoured strength to 90 tanks, while they had more than ten times as many. On 2 November the British struck again and slowly advanced through the enemy's minefields. German firepower knocked out 200 British tanks, but the Germans lost 60 tanks that they could ill afford to lose.

The Germans could not hold out much longer. On 3 November, Rommel ordered a retreat, but Hitler issued a counterorder, which forced the Germans to remain in place and suffer even more horrific losses. It would no longer be possible for the *Afrika Korps* to establish a strong defensive position within Libya. On 4 November Hitler finally and reluctantly agreed to a withdrawal, and the *Afrika Korps* rapidly retreated across Egypt and also Libya. But the British Army failed to exploit this retreat, not moving quickly enough, and the Germans succeeded in retreating as far as Tunisia. This was the beginning of the end. On 8 November Allied forces landed in Morocco and Algeria and trapped the famous *Afrika Korps* between them and General Montgomery's advancing Eighth Army.

BELOW: Surrounding Tobruk, the Germans cut off the British supply line and forced the town to surrender in June 1942. The capture of the British fortress was followed by a headlong dash for Egypt, which was only brought to a halt by the Allied defensive lines at El Alamein.

CHAPTER FOUR

EASTERN FRONT

The German attack on the Soviet Union in June 1941 marked the beginning of a long struggle for supremacy in the East. It was a struggle marked by the most ferocious fighting in history, culminating in the fall of Berlin.

The German rescue of the Italian military efforts in the Balkans and North Africa frustrated Hitler. Following the successful operations in Poland, the Low Countries and France, the Führer, despite having to abandon the invasion of Great Britain, was ready to embark upon the next phase of his plan for the creation of a new German Empire: the conquest of the Soviet Union. The commitment of German forces in Greece, Yugoslavia, Albania and North Africa forced a delay in the implementation of Hitler's plan until June 1941. Code-named 'Operation Barbarossa', the German invasion of the Soviet Union was the culmination of Hitler's desire to acquire *Lebensraum*, or 'living space', for the expanding German Reich. Hitler believed that historical precedent existed to justify German imperialism. The United States had expanded westwards across the vast North American continent, and Great Britain had amassed a great colonial empire. In order to realize its own 'manifest destiny', Germany should conquer and settle the huge stretches of land to the east.

According to the Führer's plan, the 120 divisions allocated for the offensive had less than five months in which to destroy the Soviet Army. This would be accomplished in two phases: first, a series of

LEFT: On 22 June 1941, the Nazi Germany unleashed 'Operation Barbarossa', the invasion of the Soviet Union. Although led by the Wehrmacht's Panzers, the bulk of the 120 German divisions were infantry, advancing through the Russian steppes on foot and supported by horse-drawn lines of communication.

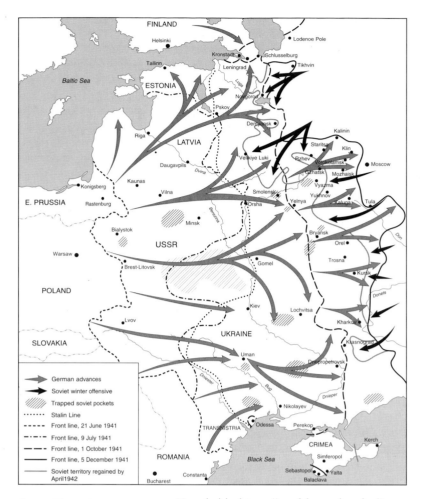

ABOVE: 'Operation Barbarossa' was carried out by three massive army groups, making a three-pronged advance into the Soviet Union. Army Group North aimed for Leningrad, Army Group Centre was directed towards Moscow, while Army Group South pushed through the Ukraine towards Rostov and the Caucasus oilfields.

Army was in bad shape. Consequently, the Soviet Government instituted a series of reforms in military organization, command structure, deployment and equipment. When the Germans attacked in 1941, however, the Red Army had not completed any of the reforms and had managed several of the planned changes incorrectly. As a result, the German forces were able to inflict heavy damages on the Soviet military.

THE RED ARMY

Perhaps one of the most important changes implemented by the Soviets in response to the Germans' 1940 victories was a return to large, combined-arms mechanized formations. In 1940 and 1942 the Soviets formed almost 30 mechanized corps that contained two tank and one motorized rifle division. Manpower and equipment shortages prevented complete implementation of the new plan. There were two causes of concern: tank shortages and the lack of medium or heavily armed and armoured tanks. In addition, by 1941 many of the light tanks were obsolete tactically and worn out mechanically. Although the Soviets had designed medium (T-34) and heavy (KV-1) tanks, there were problems with the designs. Production levels of these tanks lagged because the purges had also affected industrial management. The Soviets also lacked sufficient supplies of trucks for the movement of infantry and artillery and mines, as well as modern fighter planes.

By the summer of 1941, the Red Army still suffered from numerous deficiencies, including the use of a combination of obsolete and new weapons and troops that had not trained with the newer equipment. The 1941 invading German force, on the other hand, was highly trained, as well as being well-equipped. Operationally, the campaign was a demonstration of the height of *Blitzkrieg* tactics, particularly the encirclement battle. The failure of infantry and logistics troops to keep up with advancing panzer units, however, restricted the Germans' exploitation deep into the enemy's rear. As a result, Soviet forces had time to reorganize.

Planning to destroy the Soviet Army in a bloody *Kesselschlacht*, the German Armies unleashed *Blitzkrieg* tactics that

Kesselschlachten ('cauldron battles') to destroy forces in European Russia, and second, a decisive battle of annihilation for Moscow. Hitler was confident that the German Army's tactical excellence would allow it to achieve strategic military victory in one single campaign, or *Vernichtungsschlacht*. The previous campaigns in Poland, the Low Countries and France seemed to validate the Germany strategy; however, when implemented in 'Operation Barbarossa', *Vernichtungsschlacht* proved unattainable.

Stalin's purge of the officer corps immobilized the Red Army at the same time that Hitler's military achieved a series of victories from September 1939 until the summer of 1941. Logistical problems stemming from the occupation of eastern Poland further adversely affected the effectiveness of the Red Army. In addition, the Red Army's inability to combine formations for offensive operations became apparent during the Russo–Finnish War of 1939–1940. Although the Soviets eventually forced the Finns to agree to an armistice in March 1940, the Red

had already been tested. According to the plan, the Luftwaffe would create havoc behind enemy lines and render the Soviet air force useless. Armoured and mechanized units would penetrate and encircle the enemy army, which the infantry would then destroy.

The Soviet Army did not, however, collapse when it met the 'superior' German Army in battle. The Germans encountered an enemy army which was commanded by a leadership that was still reeling from the purges of the 1930s, but Josef Stalin expected his military forces to do the impossible: stop the German advance. Although the Soviets' military organization included over 300 divisions, none of the formations equalled a panzer group or a panzer army, which could accomplish large-scale, in-depth penetration to the enemy's rear. The Soviet mechanized divisions were unbalanced and dispersed in a way that made the concentration of these formations difficult. In June 1941 the Soviet military was definitely inferior in terms of tanks and aircraft. The Russian aircraft outnumbered those possessed by the Luftwaffe; however, because of obsolete and worn-out equipment, the Soviet air force did little to hinder German domination of the skies at the beginning of the war.

OPERATION BARBAROSSA

The plan for 'Operation Barbarossa' included a three-pronged assault on the Soviet Union: in the north towards Leningrad, in the centre towards Moscow and in the south towards Rostov and the Caucasus. When the campaign did not end in five months, the Germans began to experience logistical problems that had not been anticipated by Hitler or by the German High Command. Not only did the logistical problems hinder the German advance, but they also became critical during the harsh Russian winter of 1941.

The commencement of 'Operation Barbarossa' brought results beyond Hitler's wildest imagination. The Luftwaffe destroyed 2000 Soviet aircraft on the ground on the first day, which allowed the Germans to achieve air superiority from the beginning. Coordinating air and ground attack, the all-arms cooperation worked extremely well within the panzer formations. The coordination proved less successful in other divisions because the armoured and mechanized formations tended to outdistance the supporting infantry. As a result, the infantry generally bore the brunt of desperate enemy counterattacks. The slow movement of the infantry did not, however, prevent the Germans from advancing 322km (200 miles) in the first five days. Their vast encirclements demolished almost 100 Soviet divisions in the first week alone. By mid-July, advance German formations were less than 160km (100 miles) from Leningrad and 322km (200 miles) from Moscow.

The armies in the north and centre advanced rapidly, while Army Group South (AGS), which encountered stiff Soviet armoured resistance, moved much more slowly. Strong enemy opposition held up the Germans outside Kiev. Then Hitler made a costly mistake. In September he ordered the transfer of armour from Army Group Centre (AGC) to the south. On the one hand, the additional forces facilitated the encirclement of 600,000 Soviet troops at Kiev; on the other hand, however, AGC's advance lost momentum, which prevented it from occupying Moscow on schedule. Although Soviet forces in the centre had been on the run, the weakened AGC missed an opportunity to crush them. The Soviet forces used the time to regroup in the Soviet hinterland.

BELOW: Although the Panzergrenadiers serving alongside the Panzers were motorized, the slower pace of the following infantry divisions reduced the overall speed of the Wehrmacht's advance. The slow movement of the infantry did not, however, prevent the Germans from advancing no less than 322km (200 miles) in the first five days of the campaign.

The Soviet military scrambled to adopt measures to counter their weaknesses as enemy forces advanced deep into the Soviet Union. Two problems became noticeable immediately. First, most Soviet commanders and staff officers did not possess the skills necessary to organize the various arms and weapons effectively for defensive or offensive operations. The commanders who had survived the purges frequently received promotions that far exceeded their skill and training. Many of them failed to take the terrain or approaches that required antitank defences-in-depth into account when they deployed their troops, which caused the Soviet general staff to reprimand them. Second, the Red Army had shortages of specialized units and weapons – engineers, tanks, antitank guns, and artillery – which hindered the commanders' deployment of forces effectively in the field.

Solving these problems required major changes during the desperate struggle to thwart the German offensive. On 15 July 1941, the Soviet Supreme Headquarters (STAVKA) issued Circular No 1, which reassigned control of the specialized units to more experienced commanders and staffs, who could concentrate these limited resources to critical points on the front. The new organization of the military resulted in the formation of field armies that consisted of four to six divisions and specialized – artillery, tank, and antitank weapons – units. The STAVKA directive also reduced the amount of artillery in each division and the size of the mechanized corps.

For the rest of the year, the Red Army struggled in a conflict where the German advantages in equipment and initiative made the traditional doctrines of Deep Battle and large mechanized units ineffective. The few new tanks that the Soviets could place in the field were used as infantry support. The situation would change, however, after December 1941 when the Soviets stopped the Germans from seizing Moscow.

DRIVE FOR MOSCOW

Even though the fighting continued, 'Operation Barbarossa' was basically over by 30 September. Hitler was not, however, ready to call it off. Instead, he shifted the focus of the German offensive back to Moscow. On 2 October 1941 German forces opened a new offensive against the Soviet capital. Commencing 'Operation Typhoon' with great encirclements and tactical victories, German forces encircled most of the four Soviet armies situated west of Viaz'ma within a week, but they experienced difficulty in containing the enemy within the circle. While some enemy troops

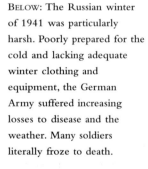

BELOW: The Russian winter of 1941 was particularly harsh. Poorly prepared for the cold and lacking adequate winter clothing and equipment, the German Army suffered increasing losses to disease and the weather. Many soldiers literally froze to death.

broke free, others began to destroy heavy weapons and vehicles to keep them out of the Germans' hands.

Overall, the German offensive initially progressed well, but winter came early in 1941 and changed the situation. The first snowfall began on the night of 6 October. Following the snow was a rainy period of mud, or the *rasputiza*, which strikes Russia each spring and autumn as the seasons change. Because of the scarcity of paved roads in those days, travel was extremely difficult during the *rasputiza*. As the attackers discovered, they would lose mobility until the ground froze solid. Experienced with the *rasputiza*, the Soviets took advantage of the enemy's loss of momentum. Although the Germans threatened Leningrad and Rostov, Stalin ordered Marshal Georgi Zhukov to leave Leningrad and organize the defence of Moscow. When he arrived, Zhukov authorized a series of spoiling attacks to divert the enemy while his forces prepared the defences outside the city.

By 27 November, however, the Germans were only a few kilometres from Moscow. By the end of November the Russian winter was in full swing. With the drastic drop in temperatures, the lack of adequate antifreeze for the mechanized formations slowed the Germans' movement even more. Hitler

failed to realize the seriousness of the situation on the Eastern Front.

RED ARMY COUNTEROFFENSIVE

While his forces reinforced their defensive positions around Moscow, Zhukov planned a counteroffensive. The Germans failed several times to regain the momentum of their advance, and each attempt took its toll in dwindling supplies and exhausted soldiers. On 6 December Soviet forces launched a massive counterattack against the overextended, exposed AGC. Although Bock requested permission to withdraw, Hitler denied his request and forced him to resign. By the end of December 1941, despite the continuing battle, the German threat to Moscow had ended. While the Soviet counterattack continued until the spring of 1942, Hitler refused to allow the AGC to surrender. The Soviets' attempt to do too much enabled the German force to survive, although Hitler concluded that his 'stand fast' order was responsible.

After their troops drove the Germans out of Moscow, the Soviet commanders returned to their organization and doctrine. By the spring of 1942, Soviet factories were producing a large number of new weapons, which were used to create new tank corps. By the summer of 1942, the Soviet commanders had

ABOVE: In the early days of 'Operation Barbarossa', the Germans caught the Soviets by surprise. Resistance collapsed in many areas, and the Germans captured large numbers of enemy soldiers. Millions of Soviet POWs were marched westwards to Germany, where they were to be used as forced labourers.

ABOVE: Soviet infantrymen, camouflaged in white to blend in with their snowy surroundings, catch an uphill ride on a T-34 tank. Large numbers of these superb fighting vehicles were used in Zhukhov's counteroffensive in front of Moscow in late 1941, supporting fresh infantry divisions arriving from Siberia.

initiated a new organization of one rifle and three tank brigades, along with supporting elements, which functioned as the mobile exploitation force of a field army. By the autumn, they added mechanized corps, which largely consisted of motorized infantry. The job of the new mobile corps, which were actually division-size or smaller, was the implementation of deep exploitations of 150km (94 miles) or more into the enemy's rear, which had been envisioned in the 1930s when the Soviets formulated a new doctrine: the Deep Battle doctrine. Earlier in 1942, the Soviets created tank armies by combined armoured, cavalry, and infantry units, but these armies did not have a common mobility rate or a common employment doctrine. Because they had not yet trained to function as a unit, the first tank armies suffered heavy losses during the summer of 1942 when they engaged the Germans in battle for the first time.

In January 1943 the Soviets finally fielded a cohesive tank army. During 1943, the Soviets organized six tank armies, which spearheaded Soviet offensives for the rest of the war. Generally, two tank corps, one mechanized corps, and supporting elements formed a tank army, which, although in reality corps size, was tank-heavy for two reasons. First, the terrain of European Russia would support tank-dominated operations. Second, because of the inexperience of Soviet tank crews and junior officers, German tank and antitank formations inflicted heavy

losses. In order to compensate for heavier losses in tanks, the Soviet armoured formations continued to contain more tanks than those of other armies.

Hitler began to plan the next big German summer offensive in the east while the Battle for Moscow still raged. On 5 April he issued Führer Directive 41, which outlined the proposed summer campaign in the Crimea, the Don Steppe and the Caucasus. Several factors, including the spring thaw, forced a delay in the operation until late June 1942. In the meantime, both sides used the time to rest, regroup and prepare for the summer campaign. STAVKA ordered the military to form 'shock' armies, with massed artillery on narrow axes in order to execute deep offensive penetrations, as well as exploitation.

TO THE OILFIELDS

Hitler had come away from the 1941–42 campaign believing that his 'stand fast' order had saved the Wehrmacht. Although Barbarossa had demonstrated the weaknesses of their strategic thinking, the Germans failed to change. They stuck to the concept of a decisive battle, of a quick victory in Russia with a knock-out blow. They also recognized the need to cut the Soviets off from their resources in the Caucasus, particularly the oil. Because of the supply situation in the south, the German High Command shifted troops from AGN and AGC to AGS, but the supply problems remained.

The German summer offensive, *Fall Blau* (Case Blue), included a deception plan. Diversionary forces would threaten Moscow in order to divert enemy troops from the south. AGS would then launch the three phases of Case Blue. During phase one, German troops would penetrate enemy defences around Kursk and conduct a typical encirclement. Prior to the commencement of the second phase, AGS would split into two army groups, 'A' and 'B'. Army Group A would conduct the main thrust by driving to and occupying the oil-rich Caucasus, while Army Group B would advance to the River Volga, north of Stalingrad.

Because the Soviets believed that the enemy would renew the assault against Moscow and Leningrad, the deception plan basically worked. The Soviets expected their formidable enemy to initiate an attempt to cut them off from the resources in the Caucasus after a new Moscow and Leningrad offensive. Despite evidence to the contrary, Stalin believed that the Germans would focus on Moscow. When the Germans opened Case Blue on 28 June with an offensive in the Kursk area, the Soviets were caught completely off-guard. The Germans achieved a quick breakthrough and commenced an offensive that seemed destined to repeat the German military performance of the previous summer. On 30 June, the Sixth Army, which was led by General Friedrich Paulus, commenced its attack south of the Kursk assault. Following Zhukov's advice, Stalin ordered a retreat. To stand fast would probably have resulted in annihilation. The Red Army retreated from the area south of Kharkov, and the Crimea fell to the Germans. Sebastopol fell after an overwhelming air and artillery attack on 4 July.

The German forces continued to achieve success in July, but they failed yet again to accomplish a decisive victory. When Hitler decided to redefine the operation's objectives, the result was that the thrust into the Caucasus came to a grinding halt and failed to result in the control of the oilfields. Then Hitler made another decision that had far-reaching and disastrous consequences: he ordered Army Group B to seize Stalingrad. For the first time, Stalingrad became the primary target for the Germans.

On 19 August 1942, the Sixth Army and the Fourth Panzer Army, under the direction of General Paulus, commenced the assault on Stalingrad. Four days later, some German troops moved into the suburbs while others reached the River Volga north of the city. When citizens from the southern part of the city began to flee to the east, the Soviet defenders panicked. Stalin ordered the Red Army to stand firm. Failure to do so would result in the transgressors' treatment as criminals and deserters. More afraid of Stalin than of the enemy, the defenders slowed the Germans' progress.

Eight days after the first shots had been fired, Zhukov became the Deputy Supreme Commander and was given the job of saving Stalingrad. He quickly

BELOW: The sheer size of the Soviet Union swallowed up each German offensive, and Soviet forces showed surprising resilience in attempting to counter the Wehrmacht's thrusts. The Red Army was still no match for German professionalism, but each battle taught the Russians more.

LEFT: German infantrymen accompany a Panzer III as the 2nd Panzer and Panzergrenadier Divisions push across the Steppes towards the town of Orel, which was taken by the Germans the previous year but lost in the Soviet winter offensive of 1941–2.

ABOVE: Wehrmacht soldiers, wade across a small river as Kleist's panzers drive towards the Caucasus.

BELOW: The autumn of 1942 saw the opening of the battle for Stalingrad. The fighting was vicious, and little mercy was shown by either side.

taking the entire city. In the meantime, the Red Army would amass a huge strategic reserve in order to lauch a well-planned counterattack that would also be well supported logistically.

Two months later the Soviets were ready to mount 'Operation Uranus'. The Sixty-Second and Sixty-Fourth Armies defended the city. General Vasili Chuikov, commander of the Sixty-Second Army, unlike many of his colleagues, demanded good intelligence, which he used to organize and move his decreasing forces when necessary to meet threats posed by the enemy. By the end of October, the battle had degenerated into a stalemate in the factory district. Regrouping his forces, Paulus launched one final attack on 9 November. Despite small successes in some areas, the Germans made little progress. The German advance ground to a halt three days later, and Soviet storm troops slowly began to retake lost territory, particularly in the centre of town and in the factory district.

On 19 November, the Soviets counterattacked north of Stalingrad and surprised the enemy. The next day, Soviet troops in the south of the city hammered the German line, which was held mainly by Romanian and Italian formations.

assessed the situation: the enemy army's limited reserves and long, exposed flanks weakened it; by implementing a pincer movement, the Soviets could surround and isolate the German forces in the city. By 13 September, Zhukov and the Chief of the General Staff, Alexander Vasilevsky, had devised a plan: 'Operation Uranus'. Sufficient forces would reinforce the defenders to prevent the enemy from

Within three days the two mobile forces advanced over 240km (149 miles) and surrounded Paulus's army. When he requested permission to surrender, Hitler ordered Paulus to 'stand fast'. On 12 December, under heavy rainfall, the attempt to rescue the trapped soldiers commenced. Initially the rescuers made steady progress, but on 23 December a tank battle with Soviet reinforcements prevented further penetration. Zhukov and the Soviet General Staff, who had anticipated a rescue effort, had made provisions to stop it. Over 60 Soviet divisions and 1000 tanks moved into place to meet the threat. On 24 December, the German rescuers, in danger of being surrounded, retreated and left Paulus and his army to their fate. The Soviets had greatly underestimated the size of Paulus's force; therefore, they had difficulty in crushing the Germans' resistance to their own destruction. Following orders, Paulus continued the fight, but on 2 September he had no choice but to surrender. The battle for Stalingrad had ended.

SOVIET SHOCK TACTICS

A year earlier when the Soviets had counterattacked a larger defensive force, the results had been disastrous. Consequently, STAVKA had issued Circular No 3, which ordered the creation of shock groups: strong concentrations of combat power that would attack on a narrow front and break through the enemy's defences. Eight months later, in Order No 306, Stalin reinforced this idea. According to Stalin's order, successive waves of infantry could not participate in shock-group attacks. Equipment and firepower shortages convinced the Soviets to maximize the effectiveness of the infantry by concentrating the infantry into a single echelon attack. By 1942 the length of the front line and shortage of troops meant that the Germans could not establish deep defensive positions. As a result, the Soviets would be more likely to break through the enemy's defences if they concentrated their infantry for a single, massive thrust. Later in the war, when both the Germans and Soviets had established defence-in-depth, the Soviets adapted their tactics to the new situation.

Following penetration of the German defences, Soviet mobile units moved through the opening to exploit and surround the enemy. Once they had accomplished a series of shallow-depth encirclements that disrupted the enemy's defences, Soviet forces would link up with other penetrating elements to move deeper into the enemy's rear positions before the Germans could withdraw and create new defensive positions. The Soviets achieved a large, operational-level encirclement for the first time at Stalingrad in November 1942. Although not entirely successful, the penetration tactics served as a model for offensive operations for the rest of the war.

The tide in the East began to turn with the Soviet victory at Stalingrad, but the fight was far from over. Despite the losses incurred at Stalingrad, both the Germans and the Soviets began to plan offensives for the summer of 1943. Although the fighting would be as fierce as it had been in the previous two years, the Soviets would have two advantages that would

BELOW: The Battle for Stalingrad began with a German attack in August 1942. The Soviets refused to relinquish control and launched 'Operation Uranus' on 19 November. Despite the fierceness of the assault, the Soviets did not regain control of the city until early February 1943.

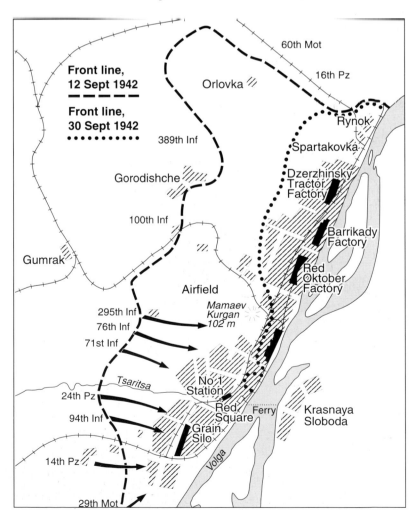

make the difference. First, unlike their enemy, the Soviets could more easily reinforce their armies and build up their supply of tanks, artillery, aircraft, weapons and other supplies. Second, and more importantly, the Soviets accurately determined where the Germans would launch their next offensive, and made the preparations necessary to thwart it. A westward bulge existed in the front lines around Kursk. The German operation 'Citadel', ordered attacks from the north and south against the salient's base to isolate and destroy the Soviet forces.

The first two days of the Battle of Kursk brought huge air and artillery bombardments, fierce fighting and a tank battle. Both sides paid a high cost on the

battlefield. The fighting culminated on 12 July with a huge tank battle near Prokhorovka. All along the front, wave after wave of Soviet tanks pummelled their enemy's forward panzer units. Both the German and the Soviet forces were exhausted after a day of extremely fierce, costly fighting. The Germans had lost almost half of the tanks they had committed to the battle, while the Soviet tank losses numbered almost 200.

THE BATTLE OF KURSK

A tense situation existed throughout the front lines of the Kursk salient. The Soviets launched a major counterattack against the Orel salient. Despite repeated requests, Hitler refused to consider a withdrawal, but finally, on 22 July, he approved an 'elastic defence', which basically allowed Model to begin to retreat. Hitler's decision showed he was willing to accept defeat on the Eastern Front, and signalled the beginning of the Germans' retreat from the Soviet Union.

Once the Soviets had stopped the German attack at Kursk, the momentum on the front began to shift. Quickly taking the initiative, the Red Army commenced attacks along the entire Eastern Front. Preceding each offensive, however, the Soviets implemented elaborate deceptions, which were frequently successful. When they were duped, the Germans concentrated their troops to thwart the fake assaults, which left them exposed in the actual area of the enemy attack.

After the deception was begun and the Germans had moved their forces, the Soviets launched a line-breaking blow against the enemy's defences. Following the creation of a hole in the Germans' line, Soviet tanks and infantry moved up to exploit the breach. Unlike the situation earlier in the war, the Soviets gradually improved their logistical situation so it no longer limited the depth of the exploitation. After the Germans regrouped and repaired their defences, the process would begin again. The Soviets, who maintained the initiative, developed numerous methods of penetration and exploitation, which kept their enemy off-guard.

The Battle of Kursk and the subsequent Soviet counteroffensives severely dented the German campaign in the East. The failure at Kursk and the loss of Kharkov were the culmination of a series of setbacks suffered by the Germans since the Soviet defeat of 'Operation Barbarossa'. Following Kursk and Kharkov, the Germans began to retreat along the entire Eastern Front. The first stage of the German collapse in the east began during the summer and autumn of 1943. The Soviets refused to relax the pressure against their retreating enemy, and the constant battles took their toll on the German infantry.

The tide that had begun to turn at Stalingrad finished turning after Kursk. The Soviets used every tool at their disposal to stop the German advance; they even used partisan forces to sabotage the enemy's efforts. In July 1941 Stalin had appealed to Soviet citizens living in occupied territory to join the effort to defeat the intruders. By January 1942, 30,000 partisans had joined the struggle against the Germans. By the summer this number had grown to 150,000. The Germans' racial policies and their treatment of the Soviets in the occupied regions persuaded many to operate behind enemy lines. By early 1943 almost 250,000 civilians had joined the partisan ranks, and the Soviet military

BELOW: German infantry equipment was often extremely good: the MG-42 general purpose machine gun was probably the best of its kind in the world, and its high rate of fire was feared by all of those who came up against it in battle.

used them whenever possible. Many operated in the forest bordering on Poland and the Ukraine. Divided into groups of 1000 men and women, they worked behind German lines to gather information about enemy troop movements, destroyed bridges, roads, railway lines, and enemy supply depots; they ambushed small enemy forces, and cut telephone lines. Those conducting operations near the front lines worked closely with the military. Beginning in 1943 the partisans engaged in intense activity against the enemy, and cost the German forces nearly 300,000 casualties. They contributed to the exhaustion and over-extension of the enemy armies, and helped hasten their collapse.

More important to their success against the Germans than the breakthrough tactics was the Soviets' numerical superiority. In addition, the Soviets implemented a variety of tactics to pierce the enemy's line, including the use of deception to draw out the Germans, who were then bombarded by Soviet artillery. The Soviet military leadership also devised different roles for heavy and

medium tanks. Although the infantry received support from heavy tanks, which attacked enemy strongholds, medium tanks frequently led the assault on the Germans' defensive positions. Combat engineers and trained infantrymen riding on the tanks provided protection against the enemy's antitank weapons. The cost of rapid penetration, however, was a high casualty rate, particularly in the combined-arms – engineers, infantry, and tanks – units. To reduce casualties, the Soviets, by 1944, relied increasingly on deception, concentration of forces, speed, and task organization. The Soviets generally used the forward detachment – a mobile, armed combined-arms unit – to lead a strike. The forward detachment's job was to capture important objectives and prevent the Germans from organizing a defence. The forward detachment did not always slow down its advance to engage the enemy. The unit left that job to the formations advancing behind it.

By 1943 and 1944, certain factors had become glaringly apparent. The Red Army fielded a much better force in

BELOW: Soviet partisans – irregular guerrilla fighters – entered the conflict against the German invaders from the earliest days of the war. Attacks led by partisans like Michail Trakhman, seen here using captured German weapons, were to become a constant thorn in the side of the Wehrmacht. Anti-partisan operations were carried out with great brutality.

1943 than it had in 1941. The army had access to more and better equipment and had accomplished improvements in tactical proficiency and combat ability. The German Army, on the other hand, was a shadow of what it had been several years earlier. Several elements of the German Army suffered decreases by 1943: shortages in manpower, weapons, and other equipment, insufficient overall training, and decline in combat ability. German commanders tended to credit numerical advantage for the Soviets' successes, not their superior breakthrough tactics. Many of the German formations remained below combat strength.

ABOVE: Dressed to blend in with the snow, Soviet guerrilla fighters cautiously move into position. By 1943, there were tens of thousands of partisans operating behind the German lines, their missions being controlled by the STAVKA. By 1944, irregular units were operating in conjunction with regular forces against the Germans.

WEHRMACHT ON THE DEFENSIVE

Troop shortages resulted in the restructuring of German infantry divisions. The Germans provided the infantry divisions with a larger proportion of fire support to counter their declining abilities. By 1944 the Germans increasingly had difficulty in containing the Soviet offensives. They could only hope to slow them down, not stop them. The Germans relied more and more on the defence-in-depth doctrine: absorb the attack, drive a wedge between the enemy's armour and infantry, and attack and destroy each in turn. Improvements in combined-arms cooperation made by the Soviets by 1944 made it increasingly difficult for the Germans to separate attacking units from each other. The decline in morale, improved Soviet intelligence, and a much more professional Red Army made preemptive German withdrawals in the face of an enemy attack much harder.

As the Soviet push depleted the enemy's infantry forces, the Germans focused on the rejuvenation of their panzer divisions. Although the panzer formations remained, the primarily tool the Germans used to counterattack, by 1944 the panzer arm could no longer remain apart from the rest of the German Army, which found itself relying more on combined-arms cooperation, from a necessity rather than a desire. Although the German commanders continued to emphasise offensive tactics, by 1943 and 1944, the German Army was no longer capable of mounting offensive operations on the Eastern Front. The advancing might of the Soviet military had forced the retreating enemy to assume the defensive.

The Soviet offensive in the summer of 1944 would ultimately decide the fate of Berlin. Larger than any of the Soviets' previous offensives had been, 'Operation Bagration' would result in the destruction of Army Group Centre and the advance of the Red Army to Warsaw. In order to divert enemy troops away from the target area, Soviet troops would attack Finland prior to the beginning of the main offensive.

On 10 June 1944 the assault on Finland began and continued through the next phase of 'Operation Bagration'. Despite German reinforcements, by late August Finland sued for peace. Soviet forces began a two-pronged attack against AGC. As a result of their rapid advance, Soviet forces inflicted 350,000 casualties on the Germans, and destroyed a total of 28 of the enemy's divisions.

The Soviets accomplished even greater successes as the centre of the German front collapsed under the weight of continuous bombardment from tank and infantry forces. Soviet pressure on the Germans continued across the Eastern Front. On 20 August over 900,000 Soviet infantry and tank and mechanized forces burst into Romania. The Romanians quickly decided not to fight, and the German situation rapidly deteriorated. By 2 September Bulgaria had withdrawn from the war against the Western Powers; still the Soviet advance continued, as forward units moved towards Hungary. German resistance in Hungary was much

TOP: Soviet infantrymen enter Berlin in April 1945. Some of the Red Army troops had fought on foot all the way from Stalingrad.

ABOVE: Soviet tank riders hitch a ride on Valentine infantry tanks supplied as Lend-Lease items by the British. For many Red Army soldiers, this was the nearest they got to becoming mechanized infantry.

armies and over 1000 tanks against 7 depleted enemy armies. Within a day, they had punctured a hole in the German line. Infantrymen and tanks pushed through the gap and advanced towards the River Oder. A day after the second offensive had begun, the first Soviet troops had pierced the enemy's defences north of Warsaw. By 17 January Warsaw had fallen. By early February they had accomplished the destruction of Army Group A, had crossed Poland and East Prussia, and had reached the River Oder. The Soviets were quick in establishing three bridgeheads across the river. One of these bridgeheads was within a distance of just 70km (43.5 miles) of Berlin.

With their treasured capital city of Berlin in danger, the Germans prepared for the fight of their lives: the defence of their homeland from the Communist hordes. The Germans strengthened their defences along the Oder front. The OKH recommended the implementation of 'defence in depth': the Germans would build several consecutive lines of defence; before the enemy's preliminary artillery bombardment, the troops in the forward-most line would fall back; after the bombardment ended, they would

stronger, though, and Soviet forces did not enter the capital, Budapest, until December. By late December, however, resistance in Hungary was virtually over.

The Soviet military machine rolled on in other areas of the front. On 12 January 1945, when the Red Army attacked along the River Vistula, it met a much weaker enemy force. Hitler had diverted formations westward for the Battle of the Bulge and for the defence of Hungary. Two Soviet offensives began around the same time. In the central part of the Front, the Soviets pitted 5 armies, 2 tank return to their positions and then proceed to stop the advance of the enemy. WIth this aim, Hitler authorized the implementation of defence-in-depth on 30 March.

The Berlin Garrison included several formations: LVI Panzer Corps, which contained 5 or 6 divisions; over 50 *Volkssturm* (home guard) divisions; and several 'Alarm Troops' formations, consisting of clerks, cooks and non-combatants. Three concentric lines of dcfcnce extended to the outer suburbs. Each ring consisted of nine defensive sectors, connected by a communications system. The military used the city's subway to move troops, equipment and other supplies without the enemy's knowledge. The heaviest defences and the largest concentration of troops protected the government sector in the centre of town. The situation was grim during the first weeks of April as the final battle neared.

BATTLE FOR BERLIN

Early on 16 April 1945 the Soviets unleashed the largest artillery bombardment of the war. Over 40,000 field guns, mortars and Katyusha rocket-launchers prepared the way for the ground forces. For 30 minutes, wave after wave of Soviet aircraft bombed German defences. Having crossed the River Oder, shouting Soviet infantrymen rushed forward and fired their guns. Soon many were engaged in brutal hand-to-hand combat with their hated enemy. What was to be the last major battle on the Eastern Front had finally, after much preparation, begun.

The rapid Soviet advance quickly bogged down as the searchlights blinded the troops. In addition, the soldiers had difficulty crossing the marshy terrain. Mechanized vehicles got bogged down and caused traffic jams and German artillery bombarded the exposed Soviet tanks. As the Soviets advanced, the Germans' resistance increased. Yet despite the fierce battle, the Soviets inched towards the German capital. After three days of intense fighting, the Soviets prepared to attack Berlin itself.

On the morning of 20 April, Soviet aircraft began bombing Berlin. During the day, Soviet artillery forces moved up. Heavy artillery barrages commenced the

next day. Ground forces moved into the city, and the fighting intensified. On 25 April Soviet forces linked up with American formations on the River Elbe, and on the same day Soviet forces cut Berlin off from the rest of Germany, raining shells on the city. Still the fight for control of the city continued. Rubble clogged up the streets and made the fighting more difficult; most of the city lacked water, gas and electricity.

Although the defenders bitterly opposed their Soviet enemy, Berlin and Germany could not be saved. With American forces nearing the city from the west and Soviet troops nearing his bunker, Hitler made preparations for the end. On 29 April, shortly after 01:00 hours, the Führer married his mistress Eva Braun. Meanwhile, the Red Army moved even closer and would soon overrun Hitler's headquarters.

On the afternoon of 30 April the Soviet assault on the Reichstag began. Despite a counterattack by German tanks, the Soviets gained control. As the red victory banner was hung from a window on the second floor of the Reichstag building, Hitler consumed his last meal. After saying good-bye to his staff, he and his new wife retired to their private rooms. A short time later they ended their lives. Despite Hitler's death, resistance would continue for a few days. On 2 May 1945 the Germans finally agreed to a ceasefire, as well as to the general surrender of all forces remaining in the city. The Soviets had won the battle for Berlin.

ABOVE: As the final collapse of the German Reich nears, Soviet bombers and IS-2 heavy tanks bombard the Reichstag building in Berlin. Following Hitler's death, the defenders of Germany's capital agreed to a ceasefire on 2 May 1945.

CHAPTER FIVE

THE PACIFIC

The war in the Pacific bore little resemblance to the European experience. Fought from island to island, through steaming rainforests and over precipitous mountain ranges, it was a war largely won by the infantryman.

World War II followed a very different path in Asia than in Europe, and historians now often consider the two to be separate, distinct conflicts. While the war in Europe was one of continental dominance fought by traditional adversaries, the war in Asia involved many, sometimes competing, motive forces. Japan, having adopted western technology and military methods in the Meiji Restoration, sought to establish an empire from the lands of rapidly collapsing China. Even as Japan sought to become a colonial power, the traditional colonial nations of Europe succumbed to chaos and defeat in World War II, allowing the Japanese to supplant their authority in much of the Pacific region. Thus the war in the Pacific was also one pitting the rise of Asian power against the legacy of European control, a theme of conflicts in Malaya and Vietnam. Finally, Japanese expansion was seen as a threat by the other great Pacific power: the United States. The resulting conflict was one for dominance over the world's greatest ocean, and the victor would emerge as the next great global superpower. Fought for reasons different to those driving the war in Europe, the conflict in Asia was a war over the future, rather than a repeat of the past.

LEFT: Pre-assault bombardments meant that American forces in the Pacific often had to advance through destroyed terrain. The war in the Pacific involved brutal fighting to winkle out fanatic Japanese defenders from their positions, often only possible through the use of flamethrowers and explosives.

69

ABOVE: Japanese infantrymen man an improvised armoured train in China in 1937. It was the expansion of Japan's imperial ambitions from mainland China into the rest of Asia that led to conflict with US and Western interests in the Pacific.

The war in the Pacific also followed a different military pattern to that in Europe, and was much more geographically and militarily diverse. In the Pacific, navies and air forces reigned supreme in a war that covered much of the globe, but often involved only tiny land areas. It was a struggle of carrier clashes and amphibious invasions launched against fanatical resistance. Even so, it would be once again the infantry, often in the form of Marines, that took and held terrain in the tropical jungles of innumerable Pacific islands and atolls.

The fighting in China and Southeast Asia, though, was different again. The war in China involved Japanese forces trying to destroy the will to resist of the world's most populous nation. In the jungles of Burma, the numerically small, but élite Japanese forces drove Allied forces back in a war of speed and stealth. These battles saw combat that would give rise to a reimplementation of irregular infantry warfare, presaging the tactics of insurgency that would come to dominate wars later in the century.

JAPAN'S CLASH WITH CHINA

Though Japan was ruled by an emperor and possessed a western form of government, by the 1930s the military was in firm control of the destiny of the country. Infused with the warrior code of *Bushido*, which stressed the martial spirit and preferred death to surrender, the military sought to expand Japan's economic base. It did this by taking control of much of China.

In the wake of the Russo-Japanese War Korea and Manchuria had fallen under informal Japanese rule, becoming chief sources of raw materials for Japanese industry. The Japanese military, though, yearned for more, and by 1930 found even their existing gains threatened by a resurgence of Chinese strength under the Nationalist warlord Chiang Kai-shek. At the same time, though, a Communist insurgency, led by Mao Tse-tung, diverted Chiang's attention and also began to set the tactical rules for nearly every insurgent revolution since. The Japanese military paid little attention to Mao, focusing instead on the threat posed to

Manchuria by Chiang's Nationalist forces. Fearing that negotiations were counterproductive Japanese military leaders in Manchuria took matters into their own hands, a move tolerated and even encouraged by their warrior code.

Without government knowledge, on 18 September 1931 Japanese military forces in Manchuria placed a bomb on an important railway near Muckden. Blaming the 'terrorist attack' on the Nationalist Chinese, the leaders of the Japanese Army in the area, known as the Kwantung Army, attacked. Ignoring subsequent government orders to desist, the Japanese military forces routed Chinese resistance and solidified Japanese control in the area, even leading a punitive expedition against a Chinese boycott of Japan in the important international port of Shanghai, laying waste to much of the city. Facing only faint international condemnation for their actions from western nations who at this point were far more interested in appeasement, the Japanese went on to

drive their forces into the Jehol and Hopei provinces of northern China before calling a halt to the offensive.

In 1937, yearning for glory and certain that their nation had to expand to survive, the Japanese military again moved against China after a minor clash of arms between Japanese and Chinese troops at the Marco Polo Bridge near Beijing. Bragging that they could conquer China in single month, the Kwantung Army moved forward, even arresting a government diplomat sent to defuse the situation.

Undertrained and poorly supplied, the Nationalist Chinese forces stood little chance against the Japanese, and by August had retreated from Beijing. Further south the Japanese laid siege to Shanghai, long a centre of Nationalist Chinese support. After seven weeks of torture the city finally capitulated, and the Japanese made ready to advance up the Yangtze River into the heart of China and towards what seemed to be an easy victory over an outmatched foe.

ABOVE: Japanese troops were very well trained and highly motivated. But their initial successes against the ramshackle Chinese Army in the late 1930s did not lead to ultimate success: indeed, at the height of the Pacific War in the early 1940s, a large part of the Japanese Army was tied down in China.

The fighting in China closely resembled that of other colonial conflicts. Highly trained and motivated Japanese soldiers with the latest equipment including light tanks and plentiful air support, easily defeated poorly trained and poorly armed Chinese troops. Utilizing superior logistic support, air power and tactical mobility, Japanese forces were able to consistently outmanoeuvre their opponents and overwhelm them once battle was joined. The Chinese, though, retained several obvious strategic advantages. Chiang and the Nationalists, though increasingly concerned with their own Communist uprising, could rely on their main weapons of numbers, time and space. If the Chinese people chose to resist, the Japanese Army was not nearly big enough to garrison the entire nation or achieve a total military victory. Thus Chiang chose to protract the war, and fight a war of attrition for which the island nation of Japan was uniquely ill-equipped.

Though the Japanese were somewhat surprised that Chiang and his forces chose to continue fighting after the fall of Shanghai, they remained quite confident, choosing to drive on the Nationalist capital of Nanking to force a decision. Chiang decided to avoid major battle but to contest the Japanese drive up the Yangtze, forcing attritional losses on his enemy. Shocked by continued resistance and taking heavy losses, the Japanese slowly drove toward their goal: supplying their forces in the main by river. In many ways the Japanese war in China was a racial war, replete with Japanese hatred for the supposedly inferior Chinese

people. Casualties taken on the drive to Nanking only served to heighten the racial animus. The Chinese still dared to resist against their rightful overlords, too ignorant to realize that the outcome of the war was a foregone conclusion. In December 1937 Nanking finally fell to the force of Japanese arms, and the pent-up Japanese hatred for their enemy found an immediate outlet. For a month Japanese forces ran riot through the city, engaging in an orgy of looting and slaughter, killing over 200,000 civilians in an atrocity so bad that even Nazi Germany's government complained.

Believing that they had made their point, the Japanese now attempted to enter negotiations with the Nationalist Chinese. Since the Japanese negotiating team demanded near-total surrender Chiang chose to fight on, retreating with his forces to remote Chunking. Here he hoped to continue the long war of attrition and pleaded for international aid. By the end of 1938, the Japanese had seized most of their military goals in China, but Japanese rule did not extend into the great Chinese hinterlands, where hundreds of millions of Chinese remained outside the sphere of Japanese control. As a result, the war in China would drag on inconclusively, with neither side able to secure victory. The Nationalists and the Communists sometimes fought hard against Japanese rule, but often squabbled among themselves. It was the vast Chinese peasantry that suffered most; millions died from famine and want caused by a nation embroiled in constant turmoil and war.

JAPAN TRIUMPHANT

Japan's success in China and obvious designs on areas in Southeast Asia and the Pacific proved quite disquieting for the western Allies. The European nations, though, could devote only scant resources to defence of their colonies in the area due to German threats to their very existence. The United States, under the leadership of President Franklin Roosevelt, recognized the threat posed by Japan, especially to US holdings in the Philippines, but could do little due to powerful forces of isolationism. Even so when Japan took control of French Indo-China in July 1941, Roosevelt took powerful economic action by announcing

BELOW: Japanese infantrymen capture Mandalay Railway Station in Burma as Imperial forces sweep triumphantly through Southeast Asia. British and Commonwealth troops proved no match for the Japanese in jungle warfare, and would not be able to fight on equal terms for at least three years.

an embargo on oil shipments to Japan. The headstrong Japanese, who received some 80 per cent of their oil imports from the United States, saw Roosevelt's act as a declaration of economic war. Threatened with economic collapse the Japanese military made ready to attack the United States. The Japanese plan of action was fairly simple. A surprise attack on Pearl Harbor, condoned by the code of *Bushido*, would cripple the US while Japanese forces seized important islands, including the Philippines, in the Pacific and the countries of Southeast Asia. Such an action would seize important sources of raw materials, making Japan nearly self-sufficient. In addition it would throw up a defensive cordon around the home islands that the US, much less its sorely-pressed British ally, would not have the willpower to test out.

On 7 December, though negotiations with the US continued, Admirals Yamamoto and Nagumo presided over the surprise carrier assault on Pearl Harbor. Though successful, the attack was, in many ways, flawed. All but two of the US battleships lost in the attack were salvageable, and the all-important US carriers were not even present at the time of the attack. Thus the attack on Pearl Harbor was not the crippling blow that Yamamoto had intended, and it only served to waken a sleeping colossus. With its mighty industrial base able to produce

in a month what Japan produced in a year, once America developed the unity required to fight a total war, the outcome was never in doubt. Even so, as the US recovered from its shock and prepared for Pacific war, but chose to concentrate its efforts on Germany, Japanese forces went from victory to victory.

In most areas of the Pacific War the Japanese were able to rely on air power and the almost uncontested might of their fleet to seize and retain the initiative. On most Pacific islands, Allied forces and their indigenous counterparts spread themselves far too thin in a vain attempt to defend everything, allowing the Japanese to achieve victories with relative ease. In two areas, though, Allied forces were deemed strong enough to hold out for extended periods, possibly even dealing the Japanese their first defeat. In the Philippines US forces under General Douglas MacArthur numbered nearly 200,000 and were augmented by a sizable air component. The perceived strength of the US force caused one reporter to comment, 'If the Japs come down here they will be playing in the big leagues for the first time in their lives.' In Singapore and Malaya nearly 60,000 British forces would defend the vaunted 'Gibraltar of the east.' Even though the defensive forces in both cases seemed impressive, in reality the Japanese held all of the advantages.

ABOVE: Using initiative and mobility the Japanese infantry were able to maintain the speed of their advance even in difficult terrain, constantly keeping Allied troops off balance. Here, part of the Japanese force heading for the Indian border makes short work of crossing the Chindwin River in Burma.

MacArthur Caught Out

In a titanic oversight, MacArthur, having been alerted of possible danger by events at Pearl Harbor, fell victim to a surprise Japanese air attack that wiped out over half of the US air strength in the Philippines in a matter of minutes. Now guaranteed air superiority, on 22 December the Japanese invasion force, consisting of two crack divisions under the command of General Homma, landed on the island of Luzon at the Lingayen Gulf. MacArthur, eschewing the plan to use his forces to defend the Bataan Peninsula, decided to meet the invasion head on. The US forces sent to meet the Japanese invasion consisted, in the main, of poorly trained and poorly supplied Filipino soldiers. Having never before witnessed combat the Filipinos found themselves hit by concentrated air, sea and amphibious assaults, and quickly broke. Leaving behind tons of critical supplies, the US and Filipino forces retreated 241km (150 miles) south to Bataan to make a final stand.

The Allied forces drew up defensive positions based on the heights of Mount Natib and awaited the Japanese onslaught. Making matters worse the defenders of Bataan were cut off from all sources of supply and found themselves starving and beset by a host of tropical diseases. In early January Homma's force struck the defences of Mount Natib but was repulsed by heavy artillery fire. Though the terrain was not suitable for tanks and made air power of little value, the Japanese were able to persevere against the staunch American defences by employing their chief strengt: the mobility and resilience of their infantry formations. American forces had thought Mount Natib to be impassable and did little to defend its rugged summit. The Japanese, though, achieved the seemingly impossible, infiltrating through the rough terrain and manoeuvring behind the American defenders. Japanese skill in jungle warfare would become legendary and often followed the pattern of the fighting on Mount Natib. Small, lightly equipped Japanese forces would seek out the path of least resistance – often hacking through trackless jungle, surviving on very little for days on end – to emerge behind an enemy who believed the area impenetrable.

Surprised by the sudden appearance of the Japanese, Allied forces now retreated further down the Bataan Peninsula to the Bagac-Orion Line. Realizing that victory in the Philippines was only a matter of time, General Homma did not make his final effort to seize Bataan until April, by which time US rations were down to 1000 calories a day, and 80 per cent of the soldiers were suffering from malaria. Reinforced by two divisions and aided by amphibious landings to the south of the US defensive line, the Japanese quickly destroyed most American resistance, leaving only the tiny island fortress of Corregidor holding out. In

RIGHT: American Amtracs – Amphibious tractors – rush forward to hit the beach at Iwo Jima. These versatile craft, able to operate on sea and on land, were critical to the success of the American 'Island Hopping' campaigns through the Central and Southwest Pacific.

LEFT: Marines move forward from the beachhead on 'Bloody' Tarawa. After victory at Guadalcanal, US forces were able to keep the Japanese off balance, attacking several important island garrisons, while leaving others to 'wither on the vine'.

the wake of a punishing artillery barrage in early May the starving survivors of Corregidor also surrendered, only to be taken into the nightmare world of Japanese prison camps.

MALAYAN CAMPAIGN

In Malaya events ran a similar course. On 8 January 1941 a daring landing by a single Japanese division pre-empted a planned British move into defensive positions in Thailand. Though the Japanese forces were weak on the ground, usually outnumbered 2 to 1, they made up for their lack of strength with mobility, surprise and command of the air and sea. British and Indian forces, though spread thinly, attempted to use the jungle terrain to their advantage in a defence of northern Malaya. The Japanese infantry, though, was lightly equipped and built for speed, making much better use of the terrain than their adversaries. Using bicycles to advance down jungle trails with great speed, the Japanese soon slipped through and around British defences in the area of Betong. Caught by surprise by the speed with which the Japanese advanced through the jungle's vastness, Allied forces soon began a southward retreat towards the fortress of Singapore. Though nearly surrounded and destroyed at the Battle of Jitra on 15 December, Allied forces attempted to form a series of defensive lines in an effort to involve the Japanese in a slow-moving war of attrition. However, the

Japanese mastery of jungle warfare again proved decisive. British and Indian forces were so thin on the ground that the Japanese never had to launch full-scale offensives into the teeth of the Allied defensive lines. Cautious Japanese probing attacks would locate the weak portions of the defensive system, sometimes only a lone jungle trail, allowing Japanese infantry to infiltrate the British and Indian positions. Again and again the Allies found their defences compromised, sometimes even discovering that the Japanese had reached the next proposed line of defences well in advance of their own retreating forces.

ABOVE: Allied forces cross a river under fire in New Guinea. Fighting in the war against Japan involved soldiers from several nations including the United States, Britain, Australia, the Netherlands and India, often supported by indigenous peoples.

ABOVE: US Marines armed with Thompson submachine guns advance slowly against fanatical Japanese resistance on Iwo Jima. The Japanese fought to the last. Fewer than 1000 of the 21,000 defenders survived to become prisoners.

By 31 January the Allied forces were finally compelled to retreat into the defensive positions of Singapore itself. The Japanese had advanced, in nearly continuous fighting, over 804km (500 miles) through some of the world's harshest terrain in under two months. Cut off from meaningful Allied support, the defence of Singapore was doomed, but the force there remained powerful. Some 45 Allied battalions manned the defences, facing but 31 Japanese battalions making ready to attack. Allied command, under General Percival, spread thin defences along the coastline of the island, holding behind a substantial general reserve that could rush to meet any oncoming threat from the Japanese.

Once again relying on speed and audacity, on 8 February the Japanese flung the majority of their attacking forces in a lightning amphibious landing against only six Australian battalions. Before the reserve forces could arrive, the Japanese were ashore and driving inland, on 15 February capturing the water supply for the city of Singapore. Faced with an urban disaster, General Percival decided to surrender. On the evening of 15 February, Percival arrived at the Japanese lines carrying a Union Jack. He surrendered his 130,000 men to a Japanese force less than half that size. The 'Gibraltar of the East' had fallen in the greatest single military disaster in British history. The Japanese had consistently used their air and naval power, as well as their superior mobility and aggressive style, in order to offset their paucity in numbers. Infantry tactics had, once again, won the day.

ALLIED COUNTERATTACK

Even as the Japanese solidified their massive gains, the United States began to marshal its forces for a Pacific-wide counterattack. Though the economic might of the US would eventually tip the balance of the war, in 1942 American forces were in many ways at a distinct disadvantage. Intelligence, though, served as a great equalizer. Having broken valuable Japanese naval codes, US naval forces surprised the Japanese on 3 June, sinking four carriers and winning the pivotal Battle of Midway. The American victory was one of the true turning points of World War II and shifted the balance of naval power back towards the United States. The Japanese fleet, though, remained powerful, especially in surface vessels, and stood ready to defend its far-flung empire. In a series of battles between near equals, Allied forces began the slow road to the home islands of Japan. US and Allied forces had to secure Australia and stabilize the long supply lines of the Pacific first, necessitating attacks along the periphery of the Japanese Empire. It was then hoped that US forces, led by MacArthur in New Guinea and Admiral Nimitz in the Pacific, could begin a series of 'island hopping' campaigns, each designed to secure naval and air bases and logistic support on the long drive to Japan.

As part of 'Operation Watchtower', designed to destroy the giant Japanese base at Rabaul, US forces began a drive up the Solomon Islands, with landings on the islands of Tulagi and Guadalcanal. Overgrown with thick jungle, Guadalcanal sported a nearly completed Japanese airfield, one that US forces would have to seize to ensure the success of their operations in the Solomons. In an operation that some dubbed 'Operation Shoestring' due to its paucity of logistic support, on 6 August the 1st Marines landed on Guadalcanal and faced no resistance from surprised Japanese construction crews, who retreated into the nearly impenetrable jungle. Quickly the Marines began to construct defensive positions around what they now dubbed Henderson Field to await an expected Japanese counterattack. The Japanese command was unsure of the nature of the unexpected Marine operation, believing that it could only be a raid, and ordered naval units to the area to crush US logistic support for the Marines. In many ways the battle for Guadalcanal would be decided by a series of titanic naval battles that swirled around the island into November as both nations attempted to supply their forces there or ferry new troops into the fray. It was, however, the Marines, undersupplied and facing heavy odds, who conquered Guadalcanal in a series of land battles that would presage the remainder of the war in the Pacific.

By the time that defeats at sea had forced US transports to flee the area, only 10,000 Marines had made it ashore at Guadalcanal with only one month of supplies, no barbed wire, no landmines and no heavy weaponry. The Marines held only a small perimeter around the airfield, leaving much of the island open to Japanese landings and resupply efforts. The existence of the Marines would be day to day and battle to battle, always on the razor's edge of annihilation. For their part, the Japanese ordered Colonel Ichiki and a force of only 1500 men to attack and destroy the Marines. Thinking the Marine force to be small and believing in the martial spirit of his own men, on 20 August Ichiki launched a headlong attack on the Marines defences along the Ilu River. Though the Japanese surged forward in suicidal waves the Marines held firm, and the next day pinned the remaining Japanese attackers onto a beach, crushing them even as Colonel Ichiki committed suicide.

Now more fully aware that the Marines were at Henderson Field in considerable numbers and were there to stay, Admiral Yamamoto ordered Guadalcanal to be retaken at all costs. The Japanese warrior code demanded that the Americans be denied victory. Thus Guadalcanal quickly became a battle that carried great meaning and would mark an even greater turning point in the Pacific war than had Midway. Utilizing night-time destroyer and transport runs dubbed the 'Tokyo Express,' the Japanese massed over 6000 men on the island under the command of General Kawaguchi. American forces, though they could rely on air support from Henderson Field, remained understrength and undersupplied due to continued Japanese naval pressure. Lulled into complacency by nearly continuous victory and convinced that his veteran soldiers could overcome the resistance of the decadent Americans, Kawaguchi

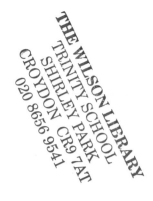

BELOW: US forces made extensive use of superior firepower in the effort to force Japanese defenders from their deeply dug-in positions. Here US Marines fire salvos of high-explosive rockets at the entrenched enemy.

made ready to assault Henderson Field without even taking the time to reconnoitre the its defences. Leaving their base near Tasimboko behind, the Japanese troops traversed the thick jungle with few supplies, sure that they would soon seize the American stores. In the defences surrounding Henderson Field the Marines realized that attack was imminent, for Marine raiding parties had discovered the Japanese build-up.

On the night of 13 September, the attack came as Japanese soldiers poured out of the jungle yelling and howling, throwing themselves at the Marine positions in human waves. Commanded by Colonel Edson, the Marines in the area resisted valiantly on what became

ABOVE: Members of the 6th Marine Division make ready to fire a bazooka at entrenched Japanese defenders on Cemetery Ridge on the island of Okinawa in 1945.

known as 'Bloody Nose Ridge.' The relentless Japanese attack forced the Marines back into their last prepared defences and the struggle became hand-to-hand in many places along the line, but the Marines held. On the next morning, now aided by aircraft from Henderson Field, the Marines put the remaining Japanese to flight, discovering that nearly one half of the Japanese who had taken part in the attack had perished. The Marines had utilized concentrated defensive firepower to hold firm against a brave Japanese attack that exhibited little subtlety. Masters of light infantry tactics and jungle infiltration warfare, the Japanese now found themselves in a war for which they were not prepared, a static war of attrition. Japanese soldiers were

discovering, as had the soldiers of World War I, that spirit had little effect on the firepower of an entrenched foe. Such battles required artillery, armour and great numbers of men, something that the Japanese lacked, but something that the United States would bring to bear in abundance as the Pacific war continued.

Having suffered a bitter defeat on land, and with the naval war slowly turning in the favour of the United States, Yamamoto decided to make one final effort to achieve victory on Guadalcanal. The Tokyo Express, though it took heavy losses, ferried in additional troops. But the United States had also reinforced its tired troops on Guadalcanal for the first time. Having gathered some 20,000 men and 100 artillery pieces, on the night of 24 October the Japanese, now under the local command of General Hyakutake, rushed forward to attack. The bulk of the human wave broke on the defences of the 1st Battalion, 7th Marines under the command of Colonel Lewis 'Chesty' Puller. Though sorely pressed, the Marines relied on the defensive prowess of their small-arms, machine gun and artillery fire to cut the Japanese down in droves. Two days later, having lost over 4000 men, Hyakutake had to admit defeat, leading his men back to their base with little hope for future victory.

Though several naval battles remained and the fighting on Guadalcanal would linger on, the decision on land had been won. By January, American forces had seized the offensive all over the island and the starving and defeated Japanese fled. On 8 February US forces entered the main Japanese base on Guadalcanal only to find it unoccupied. The United States had won its first, and possibly greatest, land campaign of the Pacific War, and the drive on Japan could now proceed in earnest. Casualties, especially for the Japanese, had been high. Of 40,000 Japanese troops sent to Guadalcanal, some 23,000 never returned from the 'Island of Death.' The Japanese had proven in earlier encounters that their light infantry, augmented by air and sea power, could outmanoeuvre and outfight forces of greater size. At Guadalcanal, though, the formula had changed, irrevocably. The US forces now had the initiative and controlled the sea and air. It would be the Japanese that tried to defend everything

against the coming onslaught, thus leaving themselves spread thin. The Americans, not the Japanese, would now mass their forces against immobile foes, using the lessons of speed and mobility that they had learned so well. In addition the Americans could rely on an almost limitless supply of military hardware. Against such odds the Japanese tried in vain to win a crippling naval victory over the Americans. The Japanese soldiers on land, though, could only fight to the death in defence of their islands in the slight hope that American resolve would soon crumble.

ISLAND HOPPING

Along with the climactic naval battles that in many ways decided the war in the Pacific, it was the American island-hopping campaign that came to epitomize the fighting in the theatre. Having seized the initiative, the American forces now began a steady drive towards the home islands of Japan, conquering islands that were needed as bases for further operations, leaving less important island unmolested, and sealing off main

Japanese bases by cutting their communications with Japan, in effect leaving them to 'wither on the vine.' In a scenario repeated over and over again in the Pacific War, US forces would pound a target island with relentless air- and sea bombardments. Under cover of this murderous fire, the Marines would hit the beaches in landing craft and in amphibious tractors. The Japanese would sometimes resist the invasion on the beaches, but would more often than not await the advancing US forces in prepared defences further inland. Realizing there was no retreat, Japanese forces would resist to the death, selling their lives dearly for their emperor. In tactics resembling those of World War I the Marines would fight from defensive emplacement to defensive emplacement, often using grenades or flamethrowers to kill the Japanese in their dug-outs and caves. Thus the war in the Pacific was one of attrition, one that the Japanese could not win, and a war that ran an inevitable course. On Beito Island in the Tarawa cluster, only 17 men of the Japanese garrison of 4500 survived the battle. On

ABOVE: Two Marines stand by as a flamethrower fires into a Japanese position during the fighting on Iwo Jima. On some of the larger islands, several Japanese soldiers held out in jungle caves for years after the war, most refusing to believe that their nation had lost.

seemingly countless islands, from Eniwetok to Saipan to Guam, the story remained the same. The battle for Iwo Jima serves to illustrate the tactics used in the island-hopping campaign.

United States forces hoped to seize Iwo Jima for use as an air base from which they could launch attacks on Japan itself. Realizing the strategic nature of the island, over 20,000 Japanese soldiers and sailors waited in defence, commanded by General Kuribayashi. Realizing he could do little but draw the battle out, Kuribayashi chose not to meet the Americans on the beaches, but to rely upon a series of defensive lines to make certain that the Americans paid a dear price in the coming struggle. With a considerable force of artillery and

antiaircraft guns at his disposal, Kuribayashi directed his men to construct some 800 pillboxes and over 4.8km (3 miles) of defensive tunnel networks into the volcanic rock of the island. When the Americans came ashore, they would be met by a punishing defence-in-depth system, once again reminiscent of the Great War, and a system which was designed to make the Americans pay for every inch of ground gained.

Against the defensive network the Americans hurled a massive storm of firepower. For 74 days US bombers struck the island, augmented by salvos of naval gunfire. It was the heaviest bombardment yet seen in the Pacific totalling 6800 tons of bombs and 22,000 rounds of heavy shells. The Japanese,

RIGHT: Tanks were not a major factor in most Pacific battles, but in some of the campaigns, they did have a role to play. Here, riflemen from the 29th Marines on Okinawa advance with a flamethrower, using an M4 medium tank as a shield against Japanese fire.

80

though, lived on in their deep bunkers awaiting the inevitable assault. On 19 February 1945 the Marines, led by the 4th and 5th Divisions, hit the beach near the imposing sight of Mount Suribachi. Initially, though several vehicles bogged down in the black sand beaches, the landing went well. As the Marines neared the higher, inland terraces of Iwo's beaches, weighed down in the clinging volcanic sand, a hail of pre-sighted artillery and mortar fire crashed down, augmented by automatic weapons fire from nearly invisible Japanese defensive works. The Marines advanced slowly against the determined Japanese resistance, but were able to get over 30,000 men ashore by nightfall.

Though the Japanese fought tenaciously the Marines inched forward, by 23 February isolating Mount Suribachi, soon reaching its summit in bitter fighting. Sometimes the Marines resorted to pouring gasoline into defensive ravines along Mount Suribachi's slopes and then setting it ablaze. At the same time the Marines also butted heads with Kuribayashi's main defensive networks surrounding the two airfields on the island. Here US soldiers had to fight their way through hellish, volcanic terrain, flushing determined Japanese from their

hideouts and often using flamethrowers to incinerate the determined defenders. In many ways there was little subtlety in the horrific fighting. Marines slogged their way through defensive features that they dubbed Death Valley and the Meat Grinder. Infantry tactics resembled that of World War I, for the Marines resurrected the artillery tactic known as the creeping barrage. Curtains of artillery fire would keep the Japanese in their pillboxes until

TOP: A flamethrowing tank lashes out at a Japanese bunker on Okinawa. The Japanese resorted to suicide attacks to defend their dwindling positions.

ABOVE: Marines, supported by a bazooka, make ready to assault a Japanese-held ridge on Okinawa.

ABOVE: Exhausted Chindit survivors aboard an aircraft returning to India. Trained to operate in the trackless Burmese jungles, the Chindits were not a notable success militarily, but they did show for the first time that European troops could more than hold their own in the jungle with the Japanese.

the Marines were upon them, blasting and burning them out at close range. Sometimes the Japanese sallied forth, either trying to infiltrate Marine lines, or launching themselves in suicide attacks. Mostly, though, they fought and died inside their defensive networks.

By the end of February the Marines had taken half of the island, and had overthrown much of the most extensive Japanese defences. Realizing that the end was inevitable, Kuribayashi radioed Tokyo apologizing for his defeat, and made ready to resist to the last. Increasingly the Japanese sacrificed themselves in suicide attacks. On 26 March many high-ranking Japanese officers, possibly including Kuribayashi himself, threw themselves at American lines in a last, desperate bid to retain their honour. Iwo Jima had been taken, but at a stunning cost. In the battle some 5931 Marines were killed and over

17,000 were wounded. Nearly 18,000 Japanese soldiers perished in the inferno, and only 216 surrendered, many of whom were gravely wounded. Several Japanese survivors, numbering in the thousands, remained hidden in their defences and doggedly resisting US victory. Some of them remained until several years after the close of the conflict, believing that the war in the Pacific was still raging.

Thus the American ring began to close around Japan, culminating in dramatic naval victories surrounding the Philippines, the invasion of Okinawa and the dropping of the atomic bomb. Though naval battles, from the Coral Sea to Leyte Gulf dominated the story of the Pacific war it was, once again, the infantryman that took and held land, enabling the American naval and air forces to advance. The fighting on the islands of the Pacific was of a grim, attritional nature. Relatively small numbers of Marines and US soldiers advanced from island to island, scoring their first major victory at Guadalcanal. Unlike the mechanized wonders that were European armies, the Marines slogged slowly forward, facing fanatical Japanese resistance and retaliating with brute force. Though the terrain of the Pacific was quite different, the fighting in those islands would have been quite familiar to a soldier who had fought in the Great War.

IRREGULAR WAR IN BURMA

Pushed back to the Indian border, the British sought methods by which to strike back at the Japanese, both to pre-empt any new Japanese offensives and to herald their return to Burma. Such a move would also do much to re-open supply lines to Nationalist forces in China and would receive aid from American and Chinese forces under the command of General 'Vinegar Joe' Stillwell. On 21 September 1942 British and Indian forces, under the overall command of General Wavell, pressed forward in the Arakan Campaign, but met little success. One aspect of the campaign, though, received much attention and helped to lay the foundations for the jungle fighting which was later seen during the war against counterinsurgents in Vietnam.

General Orde Windgate, having learned the principles of guerrilla warfare from Jewish insurgents in Palestine, led the training of some 3000 British, Ghurka and Burmese soldiers, hoping to lead a

ABOVE: Chinese irregular forces cross the Salween River in Burma. Chindit operations supported the Chinese/American campaign to take northern Burma.

BELOW: Chinese regular troops load an 82mm (3.23in.) mortar during assault on Japanese positions on Pingka Ridge in 1944.

ABOVE: A British infantryman of the Fourteenth Army in Burma. British forces developed jungle fighting skills which would influence insurgency fighting for the next three decades, right through the Vietnam War.

RIGHT: Under the command of General 'Bill' Slim, the British Fourteenth Army in Burma outmanoeuvred and outfought one of the largest Japanese armies outside of Manchuria.

could act in units of brigades or larger, often melted into companies and even squads to facilitate stealthy movement through the enemy-held terrain. On 8 February 1943, with Wavell's reluctant blessing, the Chindits advanced over the Chindwin River into Burma and succeeded in catching the Japanese completely unaware. The Chindits blew up bridges and severed the main Japanese rail route in more than 30 places. Having attracted the attention of the Japanese, Windgate's forces then simply melted into the trackless rainforest. One Japanese general stated, 'If they stay in the jungle, they will starve.' However, the Chindits survived, living off the land and off air drops, and they emerged only to cause yet more havoc. Eventually the Japanese had to devote two whole divisions to the Chindits' destruction.

However, Orde Windgate soon made a critical error. He moved his forces out of their jungle hideaways and out of the range of Allied air drops, in an ill-fated effort to link up with British ground forces further south. Without cover and without supplies, the Chindits found themselves sorely pressed by persistent Japanese attacks. Suffering heavy losses, on 24 March Windgate received orders to retreat. Once again relying on stealth, the Chindits broke down into small units and then exfiltrated through the encircling Japanese forces.

'long-range penetration' raid into Burma which was aimed at disrupting Japanese communications and logistics. Highly trained and motivated, the Chindits, as they came to be known, practised the art of living off of the land in jungle terrain, planning only to be supplied by air drops. Additionally the Chindits, though they

Forced to retreat 241km (150 miles) through rugged terrain, always under the threat of enemy attack and with no supplies, the Chindits lived off the land and had to use all of their jungle skills to survive the trek. Many died on the journey and most considered their mission a failure. However, a small unit had proven that it could, with no vulnerable supply lines, spread havoc deep into enemy territory. With better planning, the Chindits were certain that they could nearly paralyze Japanese movements, and force the Japanese to devote many front-line units to defensive roles in the rear, serving to help bring balance to the war.

IMPHAL AND KOHIMA

In March 1944 the Chindits struck again. Along with a thrust by Merrill's Marauders, American and Chinese soldiers using similar tactics, the Chindits hoped to seize control of northern Burma. At the same time the Japanese went forward into their long-awaited 'U-GO Offensive' aimed at overthrowing British India. Three brigades of Chindits entered Burma by land and by glider landings near the Irrawaddy River at a site dubbed Broadway.

With their airfield connection to the outside world secure, the Chindits set up a series of defensive patrols and also set out to besiege the critical Japanese communications hub of Indaw. At the same time, Merrill's Marauders pressed down the Mogaung River valley towards the major Japanese hub of Myitkyina. Sensing the danger General Honda, the Japanese commander in the area, began to remove troops from the front lines in India to deal with the threat to his lines of communication. The Japanese focused their attacks on the Chindit supply bases, including the Broadway airfield.

In battles that presaged tactics used in Vietnam, the Chindits sent patrols out into the jungle from their secure base area, detecting Japanese movements before they became a definitive threat. In addition, forward air controllers worked to call down punishing air attacks on the unsuspecting Japanese. Both sides manoeuvred for tactical supremacy, but the Chindits were successful in defending their bases and in April they succeeded in

occupying Indaw, where they destroyed massive caches of Japanese supplies.

After Windgate's untimely death, the Chindits, having caused much havoc, moved with Merrill's Marauders to capture Myitkyina and succeeded in their efforts to free northern Burma from Japanese control. Meanwhile, the Japanese offensive against India collapsed, leading to a general Japanese retreat in the area. The Allies now shifted over to the general offensive in Southeast Asia driving towards victory even as naval power in the Pacific broke the back of the Japanese empire. The tactics on the islands of the Pacific, though they had

involved modern amphibious landings, had closely resembled the brutal infantry advances of the Great War. In Burma, though, the British and Americans had turned the rugged terrain into an advantage. They relied on forward air bases and jungle fighting skills to act as force multipliers for their numerically weak units. The result was a resounding victory. Further to the east, in Vietnam, Ho Chi Minh and his Viet Minh were the only forces now standing against Japanese rule. As World War II ended, the Viet Minh seized control, only to face the return of their French colonial masters. It was in that resulting, unexpected war where the irregular tactics of jungle warfare which had been pioneered by Windgate and Merrill would come to their final fruition.

ABOVE: Fighting through the jungle, often supplied and supported solely by air, British and American Chindits and Marauders developed many of the techniques used by the Special Forces in Vietnam.

CHAPTER SIX

AFTER D-DAY

Germany's high-water mark came in 1942, but from that point on, there was nowhere to go but down. Hitler's Third Reich was at war with the world's most powerful nations, and retribution would not be long in coming.

Despite some setbacks, the Germans had amassed a large number of successes from the time of Hitler's ascension to power until the summer of 1942. By that time, the Germans, who were engaged on several fronts, began to suffer a series of defeats. The beginning of the end in North Africa came in October 1942 when the British achieved victory in the Battle of El Alamein. Seven months later the conflict in North Africa ended with the German surrender in Tunisia. In 1943, the Soviets handed the Germans several defeats in the east; the two most devastating defeats occurred at Stalingrad and Kursk. Following their defeat at Kursk in the summer of 1943, German forces began the slow retreat back to Germany.

Sicily became the next target of a joint British–American effort. Before the campaign started, the Allies launched a major air assault against the enemy's island airfields. Code-named 'Operation Husky', the invasion of Sicily began on 10 July 1943 as seven Allied divisions landed on the southeast corner of the island. The largest amphibious landing of the war included two armies, the British Eighth Army, commanded by Montgomery, and the US Seventh Army, led by General George Patton. While more troops landed later on

LEFT: The beginning of the end for Nazi Germany came in Tunisia, soon after the disaster at Stalingrad. British and Commonwealth troops, veterans of years of desert war, linked up with fresh American divisions from Algeria to force Panzer Army Afrika into a final defeat. The next step was to attack the Axis in Europe.

Normandy, on the first day of 'Husky', more soldiers came ashore than was the case on the first day of 'Overlord'. The Allies expected little resistance on the island because of the Italians' low morale and the small number of German defenders and, although they encountered stiff German defensive efforts, the Allies gained control of Sicily by the middle of August. Because of the methodical way in which Montgomery managed the campaign, however, a large number of German troops succeeded in escaping to Italy before they could be captured by the Allies.

ON TO ITALY

The next logical step after the fall of Sicily was Italy. As had been the case in North Africa and Sicily, the toughest resistance in Italy would come from the Germans, not the Italians. Although the Italians accepted the conditions for armistice on 1 September, two days later the Eighth Army came ashore on the toe of Italy. On 9 September a joint British–American force landed south of Naples in the Gulf of Salerno.

Code-named 'Avalanche', the invasion of Salerno nearly failed. Under General Mark Clark's direction, two British divisions and an American infantry division landed on opposite sides of the River Sele. Because of the steep terrain behind the invasion beaches, the defenders, entrenched on the high ground, had a definite advantage. While the German 16th Panzer Division defended the beach, Allied troops fought their way on to the shore. By 12 September, the Allies had established a narrow beachhead. Because the two forces had not yet linked their positions, they were extremely vulnerable. On 13 September parts of four panzer and panzergrenadier divisions counterattacked the gap between the British and American positions. Despite the Allies' critical situation, stiff fighting and the timely arrival of reinforcements to the beachhead saved the day.

The Germans made the Allies fight for every step they took on Italian soil. Not willing to relinquish control of Italy to the enemy, the Germans constructed three lines of defence. The Gustav Line stretched across the peninsula south of Monte Cassino; the Gothic Line traversed the country north of Arezzo; and the Alpine Line protected the area north of the Verona–Trieste line. Because of the Germans' strong defensive positions south of Rome, the Allies advanced very slowly, which caused them to change their objective. Although the Italian campaign seemed to have become a strategic dead end, the Allies did not abandon it. Instead, they planned to use it to tie down German forces and prevent their transfer to other theatres, particularly the Eastern Front or France.

The Italian campaign did allow the Allies to accomplish another objective: the refinement of the fighting methods that they had developed in North Africa. They recognized the importance of achieving air superiority before launching a land battle, and they worked on improvement of their artillery tactics. In addition, the Allies developed better ground-air liaison and emphasized greater combined-arms cooperation, especially infantry-tank cooperation. Although these changes and improvements would prove useful in the Northwest Europe campaign, numerous factors – slow advances and poorly coordinated, firepower-laden battles – impeded the Allies' progress in Italy.

British and American military officials learned much from the amphibious landings on Sicily and Italy. They would apply the lessons they learned when planning their next major amphibious assault, the invasion of Northwest Europe. The Germans, who were expecting the Allies to come, had begun to construct the Atlantic Wall, a series of defences meant to thwart an enemy assault. The Allies had been planning a cross-Channel invasion for some time, and many factors determined where and when the attack would come. British and American military leaders had no illusions about the cost – in terms of men, weapons, ammunition, equipment, food, and other supplies – of a campaign against German forces. The campaign would have to include an amphibious landing in a well-defended region followed by a thrust to drive them back into Germany and then achieve an unconditional surrender.

PLANNING THE INVASION

By January 1944 the Combined Chiefs of Staff had chosen an invasion site – Normandy – and also established the command structure for the invasion force. While General Dwight Eisenhower was the overall commander of the operation and of Supreme Headquarters Allied Expeditionary Force (SHAEF), Montgomery, the commander of 21st

LEFT: Although the Italians surrendered in September 1943, the Allies did not easily gain control of the peninsula. The Italian terrain is far from easy to fight through, and every major town had the potential to bog down any advance for weeks or even months, as each had to be cleared in fierce house-to-house, or more accurately, ruin-to-ruin battles.

CHAPTER SEVEN

INFANTRY AFTER 1945

With the end of World War II, dormant differences between the Allies were free to come into the open. Rivalry between East and West was to lead to a new kind of struggle between two systems of living: the Cold War.

In 1945 World War II finally came to an end. The Germans surrendered in May, and the Japanese officially in September. The cost had been high. Because of the Japanese soldiers' willingness to fight to the death – to surrender was dishonourable – President Harry S. Truman made the tough decision to use the newly perfected atomic bomb. The crew of the Enola Gay dropped the first bomb on Hiroshima on 6 August. Three days later a second atomic bomb fell on Nagasaki. Despite the military's desire to continue fighting, Emperor Hirohito ordered his advisers to accept America's terms for surrender, provided he could retain a ceremonial position. On 2 September 1945, the Japanese signed the surrender. The war was over.

Although the war had ended, peace did not return. A clash between the interests and ideas of East – the Soviet Union – and West – the United States and Britain – quickly dominated international relations. A series of disagreements between the United States, Britain, and the Soviet Union led increasingly to distrust. As tensions grew, the alliance that had existed because of a common enemy began to crack, and a different sort of war broke out between the East and the West: the Cold War. Lasting from 1945 until 1990, the

LEFT: The life of the infantryman has changed more since the end of World War II than in any other period of history. The process of mechanization which began during that conflict has been completed, the foot soldier now being invariably conveyed to battle in armoured personnel carriers like these American M113s.

103

Cold War was characterized by ideological differences, threats, 'brinkmanship', 'containment', hot and cold periods, and a series of crises in Europe, Asia and the Middle East.

The atomic bomb changed the nature of militaries after the war. Both the fear of and the desire to produce atomic bombs drove the leading powers of the world – particularly the United States and the Soviet Union – to embark upon an arms race and to engage in atomic bomb diplomacy. The distrust and disillusionment between East and West resulted in ever-increasing tensions. Questions about the role of conventional troops and the nature of future wars arose. Because both countries wanted to avoid nuclear conflict, they ultimately developed strategies based upon the concept of limited war.

Two trends permeated the major powers' armies in the post-war period and suggested that mechanized armour was not the solution to future combined-arms combat problems. Many strategists believed that the atomic bomb made traditional land warfare obsolete. Other strategists expected any future land combat to be radically different from what had been experienced during the war. In the late 1940s, many in the United States military believed that in the future the infantry would protect strategic bomber bases and 'mop up' enemy forces dispersed by nuclear attacks. Although they later came to recognize the need for land forces, many strategists believed that nuclear weapons would render the large and conventional armies unnecessary.

Both the United States and the Soviet Union realized that a nuclear conflict between them would be suicide; therefore, the two nations participated in a series of 'proxy wars,' in which they supported smaller countries engaged in conflicts. These proxy, or national liberation wars, because they engaged in guerrilla tactics and stressed political objectives, challenged the use of conventional mechanized armies. Western armies had two ways in which to meet the challenge of national liberation wars. They could either try to use their conventional forces in an unconventional-type conflict, or develop light infantry units at the expense of armoured weapons. While Western armies debated the options and underwent a series of changes, the Soviet Army used the period between 1945 and 1970 to eliminate its technical disadvantages in conventional combat.

After World War II, the Soviet Army underwent four periods of doctrine and organization. Between 1945 and 1953, although they maintained the tactical and operational doctrines and organization used during the war, they disbanded part of their forces. The development of nuclear-equipped arms relegated conventional forces to the background between 1953 and 1967. The desire to construct an armour-heavy force that could survive and exploit a nuclear attack took precedence over the maintenance of a Soviet Army trained in combined-tactics. From the late 1960s until the mid-1980s, however, Soviet attention returned to conventional forces. The Soviet Army prepared a doctrine for a combined-arms mechanized conflict that might or might not be used in conjunction with nuclear weapons. Finally, after the mid-1980s, two factors – the war in Afghanistan and the development of new weapons – dictated that a thorough reorganization of the Soviet Army be conducted.

Because it did not possess any nuclear weapons, in 1945 the Soviet Army developed a doctrine to enable its conventional forces to counter any eventuality in Europe. While they constructed a doctrine based on the reality of the mid-1940s, the Soviets also attempted to develop their own nuclear weapons. By 1948, however, Stalin reduced the size of the military by more than half, but at the same time, he authorized an increase in the number of armoured and mechanized formations. At the same time that the military increased its mechanization, Soviet strategists created a new doctrine. In 1949, after they detonated their first atomic bomb, the Soviets' emphasis on the use of conventional ground forces for national security declined.

SOVIET MODERNIZATION

Following Stalin's death in 1953, the Soviets began a 'Revolution in Military Affairs' and focused on nuclear weapons and electronic and communications improvements. Field Marshal Georgi Zhukov, who desired to adapt Soviet ground forces to the realities of nuclear warfare, received permission to reorganize the military. To improve command and control and provide protection against nuclear weapons, Zhukov reduced unit size and ordered better armour. With the reorganization came a doctrine that dictated a nuclear strike followed by exploitation by mechanized, armour-heavy forces. Combining new equipment and reduced size, all ground units became motorized and, in numerous instances, mechanized. By 1959 the Soviets demonstrated their

BELOW: On exercise in 1952. After helicopter-borne infantry units have established a beachhead on the far side of a river, the remaining force cross the river in assault boats, while engineers set up a pontoon bridge which will allow vehicles to move across the water obstacle.

reliance on nuclear capabilities with the creation of the Strategic Rocket Forces. In the early 1960s, Soviet commanders, driven by the necessity for rapid exploitation and Deep Battle, examined the possibility of limited use of air mobility. In addition, because ground forces had been relegated to a 'mopping-up' role, the infantry experienced a reduction in size, and conventional forces in general took a back seat to the more important nuclear-strike capabilities possessed by the military.

The removal of Nikita Khrushchev from power in 1964 opened the way for changes in the Soviet military. Military leaders debated the future direction of the armed forces, particularly in light of the new American doctrine of flexible response. Recognizing that future wars would not be fought in the United States, the military emphasized forces capable of fighting a wide spectrum of possible conflicts: terrorism, guerrilla warfare, a conventional conflict, or a nuclear war. Acknowledging that it was not realistic to have only one option to an external military threat, Soviet officers returned to the possibility of conventional combined-arms warfare. They analyzed the memoirs of World War II senior commanders and focused on two concepts – mobile group and forward detachment – which were essential to their mechanized exploitation and pursuit methods. By the 1970s the organization of the Soviet military reflected the evolution of military doctrine. Mechanized infantry and conventional artillery battalions became re-attached to tank regiments. The Soviets' doctrine and organization of combined-arms combat had come 'full circle' by the mid-1970s and incorporated improved armoured fighting vehicles and helicopters into the 'Deep Battle' and mechanized combined-arms doctrine.

RIGHT: Although poison gas was not used in World War II, the threat of Nuclear, Biological and Chemical warfare (NBC) was taken very seriously during the Cold War. Seen here in November 1956, members of the US Army Chemical Center in Edgewood, Maryland, wear NBC masks as they make a field demonstration of a new resuscitator that was designed at their facility.

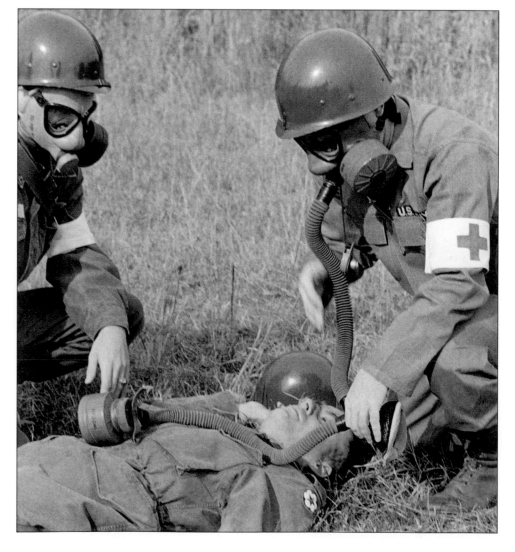

Unlike their Soviet counterparts, American field commanders were not completely satisfied with the organization of the United States military in 1945. An analysis of the performance of the triangular infantry division suggested that each division should have armour that would support infantry attacks and function as the army's primary antitank weapon. The incorporation of this organization, however, would tie the tanks to the infantry and prevent them from attacking and exploiting the vulnerabilities of the enemy. By 1946, the number of armoured infantry battalions in each armoured division increased from a total of three, to four.

DOWNSIZING THE US MILITARY

Two factors prevented the reorganization from having a large impact on the American land forces. First, demobilization after the war reduced the overall size of the military. Second, the emphasis of military doctrine shifted from combined-arms warfare to nuclear warfare. In general, because of the United States' initial monopoly on nuclear weapons, only army commanders envisioned the importance of having combat-ready forces. Despite some changes in the organization and size of the ground forces, the military doctrine emphasized the United States' ability to

launch an air-atomic campaign against Soviet targets to shock and unhinge the Soviet Government. Events would force the United States to rethink its doctrine.

One of the major disagreements between East and West emerged even before Hitler had been defeated: the nature of the post-war world. Stalin proved willing to be the first to challenge the situation by commencing a period of expansion beginning in the spring of 1946. Although the United States and Britain willingly conceded the Soviets' right to a sphere of influence, they feared the spread of world Communism, which did not recognize borders. In response to the apparent Soviet threat, the United States developed the policy of containment. The United States would take a series of steps to 'contain' the spread of Communism and the Soviets' influence. In 1947 President Harry Truman announced the commencement of the Marshall Plan, which would provide the financial means to rebuild Europe. Stalin countered with the Molotov Plan, which would help rebuild Eastern Europe.

The United States planned to use the atomic bomb to 'contain' the Soviet Union. In mid-1947, the Joint Chiefs of Staff developed a war plan – 'Broiler' – which incorporated the bomb for a first strike against Soviet political targets. In the spring of 1948 Truman was able to

ABOVE: During the Cold War the US Army established training units equipped with enemy weapons, initially to establish their capabilities and then train regular units in how to counter them. 'Opfors' members are seen here with an RPG-7 antitank grenade launcher, an AK-47 assault rifle, a flamethrower and a T-54 main battle tank.

test the atomic strategy when the Soviets cut rail and road traffic to West Berlin. Although he did not deploy bombs to air bases in Great Britain, Truman implied that he had. The blockade ended over a year later without the use of nuclear weapons. Although the United States continued to build atomic bombs and develop war plans, such as 'Fleetwood,' the military did not rule out the possibility of a limited conventional campaign. A limited conventional campaign would, however, follow on from an atomic attack.

In 1949, when the Soviets exploded an atomic bomb, the situation changed. By the end of the year, United States' military strategists, placing larger emphasis on the bomb, developed a new war plan: 'Offtackle'. In the early 1950s the US continued to fund the atomic bomb program at the expense of conventional forces. A further complication arose when the Soviet-equipped North Korean Army invaded South Korea in June 1950. America's commitment to the fight in South Korea demonstrated the military's deficiencies. Not only did the troops lack training and combat power, but the Army's force structure also failed to match its doctrine. The need to correct the military's problems and the involvement

on the Korean peninsula resulted in a temporary increase in both the Army's budget, and its size.

THE NUCLEAR SHADOW

A new administration came to power in the United States when Dwight Eisenhower was elected president. Eisenhower and his administration developed a national strategy based on 'massive retaliation' with nuclear weapons. As had been the case for the Soviet Army, the American Army had to devise a doctrine and a structure for ground forces to function on a nuclear battlefield. While maintaining efficient command and control, the doctrine had to demonstrate an ability for greater dispersion and flexibility. The Army had to be prepared for deployment anywhere in the world on short notice. These factors dictated the tactical structure of the army: small, dispersed units that were not nuclear targets, self-sufficient when isolated, and self-supporting without vulnerable supply lines. The result was the 'Pentomic Division', five units within a division that could function on either an atomic or a conventional battlefield. Because of the need for mobility, the 'Pentomic Division' would include a helicopter company and numerous APCs (armoured personnel carriers) in an infantry formation. The pentomic changes had the most effect on infantry units. By 1959 the United States Army, which had undergone major structural and operational changes, was theoretically ready to meet the demands of nuclear warfare.

The early 1960s brought a new administration and a new military doctrine: 'flexible response'. Under the new doctrine, the military would field forces that were capable of fighting a wide range of wars: terrorism to full-scale conventional to nuclear. Because the 'pentomic division' seemed ill-suited to the new doctrine, the Kennedy administration authorized studies into the reorganization of the army. Under the new organization, different types of Reorganization Objectives Army Divisions (ROADs) would operate from the same base. The largest manoeuvre organization with a fixed structure became the battalion. The advantage of the ROAD division was its ability to

BELOW: Post-war Soviet tactics emphasized surprise and speed of movement. Red Army soldiers, wearing the standard leaf-pattern camouflage uniforms of the 1970s, practise deploying from a BTR-152 armoured personnel carrier.

LEFT: Observing the placement of their forces, these Czechoslovakian officers make a final review of their tactical plans before commencing the manoeuvres. Behind them can be seen the Czech-built RM-70 versions of the standard Warsaw Pact 122mm multiple rocket launcher.

adjust its structure to the assigned mission. Consequently, depending upon the threat, the army could deploy either a particular type of division – armoured, mechanized, conventional infantry, airborne, or air mobile – or various kinds of divisions. The drawbacks of using ROAD divisions were some inefficiency and coordination problems.

The United States and Soviet Armies were not the only ones to undergo changes in doctrine and organization during the Cold War. For the 10 years following the formation of the North Atlantic Treaty Organization (NATO), however, the armies of most European nations made few alterations to their existing structure and doctrine. Until 1960 the military policies of the Western European states were similar to those of the post-World War I period. Most European countries did not want to fund new weapons systems. Following 10 years of occupation, West Germany was allowed to re-arm because of the East-West conflict. The Bundeswehr (Federal Armed Forces), because of the inability to mechanize all formations, provided front-line units with different equipment and tactics from other units. Both the French and the British Armies developed three elements. First was a fully mechanized force that had the responsibility of defending Central Europe. The second element was a less well-equipped conscript and reserve force that served at home. The final

element was a lightly equipped, strategically mobile unit that was well-trained and that would participate in conflicts outside the European sphere.

In the 1960s changing circumstances led the British and French armies to shift their attention to the defence of Europe. Because Britain, France, and West Germany focused on the concept of combined arms ('all-arms cooperation') as a principle of tactics, their militaries demonstrated similar large-unit organization with fixed, combined-arms structures. By 1961, with the end of the Algerian War, the French Army turned again to mechanized operations and organizations. In the 1960s and the 1970s the French Army developed the organic combination of different arms within one battalion. The culmination of combined-arms experiments was the mixed or 'tank-infantry' battalion. While

ABOVE: Introduced by the Soviet Army in the 1960s, the BMP was the world's first infantry fighting vehicle. Designed to take a squad into action, it differed from earlier APCs in its ability to provide powerful fire support, as well as its ability to engage enemy tanks with its AT-3 'Sagger' guided missiles.

France took the lead in forming mixed battalions, West Germany began to create mounted infantry integrated with armour. Unlike the Americans who built armoured carriers for transporting infantry who would disembark to fight, the Germans developed infantry fighting vehicles (IFVs) in which the infantry would ride and fight. Other NATO nations, as well as the Soviet Union, copied both the concept and the design of the IFVs. By the late 1970s, however, because of the development of higher-velocity tank guns, infantry formations were even more vulnerable to armoured attack than they had been in 1943.

Following World War II, as the division between East and West widened, both sides formed organizations for collective security. In April 1949 the Western powers, including the United States, the United Kingdom and Canada, signed the North Atlantic Treaty, which created NATO. West Germany became a member in 1955. In response, the Soviet Union, East Germany, and other Eastern European countries signed the Warsaw Treaty of Friendship, Cooperation, and Mutual Assistance in May 1955. The treaty had provisions for a unified military command and for the maintenance of Soviet forces within the territories of the participating states.

NATO DOCTRINE

The main goal of NATO was to unify and strengthen the military response of the Western Allies in the event of an invasion by the Soviet Union and its Warsaw Pact Allies. The purpose of such an invasion would be the spread of Communism. In the early 1950s, because the Soviet Union had much larger ground forces, NATO counted on the possibility of massive United States nuclear retaliation to deter aggression by the Soviets. In 1957, to supplement this policy, NATO deployed US nuclear weapons in Western European bases; many of them were situated in West Germany and pointed to the East. The nuclear weapons would remain under the control of the United States. Throughout the 1950s and 1960s, in addition to increasing its nuclear arsenal, NATO forces systematically developed. Despite deficiencies in size when compared to that of the Soviet military, the sophistication of the NATO units' weaponry and training made them equal in strength to their Soviet adversaries.

As the Soviet Union developed nuclear weapons, it positioned them in Eastern Europe and faced them to the West. Although the situation on the border between Western and Eastern Europe remained tense during the 1950s, 1960s and into the 1970s, other events, such as the Korean War and the Vietnam War, lessened the chance of a nuclear conflict.

The end of the Vietnam War began a period, from 1973 until 1989, that was dominated by confrontation between NATO and the Warsaw Pact. Throughout the 1970s, the Warsaw Pact, which was dominated by the Soviet Union, turned to confrontation because of suspicions of aggression towards the East by the West. In addition to building up its conventional forces, the Warsaw Pact developed and deployed intermediate-range nuclear weapons, including the SS-20 fully mobile missile system. An intermediate-range nuclear

BELOW: On 27 October 1956, a revolt against Soviet control erupted in Hungary. Soviet tanks moved into Budapest as the Red Army quickly quashed the rebellion.

missile force (INF) race was the result, and it was won by NATO, who stationed over 570 new Pershing II and ground-launched cruise missiles in Western Europe, particularly in Western Germany and the United Kingdom. The United Kingdom also began to upgrade its nuclear arsenal with the Trident D5 submarine-launched ballistic missile (SLBM) system. The decision by NATO to increase its nuclear arsenal in Europe sparked a series of protests by various groups, such as the Campaign for Nuclear Disarmament (CND).

The protests did not result in the removal of the missiles or stop the deployment of new missiles. Cruise and Pershing II missiles, which began arriving in Europe in November 1983, re-established NATO's ability to threaten limited nuclear retaliation that was designed to stop short of starting a global nuclear war. The new missiles reduced the time it would take to strike a target. The new NATO strike capabilities had an impact on Soviet military doctrine and strategy. Endeavouring to stress the weaknesses of NATO, the Soviets began to re-emphasize the 'Deep Battle' and 'Deep Operations' doctrines in the 1970s, which they demonstrated publicly. In 1981 the Warsaw Pact conducted the 'ZAPAD 81' manoeuvres in the Baltic States and Poland. The Soviets also developed war plans for multiple 'echelons' of Soviet and Warsaw Pact reserve forces, which would advance through Poland and East Germany. The plans suggested the very real possibility of the Soviets breaking through NATO's Central Front forces in a few days without using nuclear weapons.

The United States led the response by NATO, which was to develop doctrines predicated on technology and skilled manoeuvres, not manpower. In doing so, NATO forces would maintain a credible conventional defence of the Central

TOP: To prevent the escape of its citizens, the East Germans fortified the border with the West and built the Berlin Wall. Here, an East German work party examines the 'Death Strip' near Checkpoint Charlie.

ABOVE: Guarded by US troops, Checkpoint Charlie on the Friedrichstrasse, Berlin, was one of the few points through which people could travel between East and West.

ABOVE: Reconnaissance and intelligence-gathering are vital to the success of any military operation. Originally performed by the cavalry and then by reconnaissance vehicles, like this British Army Fox, the mission is now mainly performed by airborne assets like the Anglo–French Gazelle utility helicopter.

Front. First proposed in 1979, the NATO plan was called 'FOFA' (Follow On Forces Attack). Under 'FOFA,' NATO would develop surveillance and reconnaissance systems to 'see deep' into the enemy's rear positions. The goal was to identify ground- and air targets. After the targets were identified, aircraft, missiles and long-range artillery would 'strike deep' against the Warsaw Pact reserve echelons in order to prevent them from reaching the battlefield. As part of their NATO contribution, the United States and British military adopted ideas of manoeuvre, along with 'FOFA', during the 1980s.

During the Cold War, wars occurred more often and lasted longer than they had in the first half of the century. Of the 32 major and 75 minor conflicts that had occurred by the late 1980s, many had nothing to do with the Cold War. Some of the most significant wars of the post-World War II period took place in the Middle East. After 1945, colonial powers lost their hold on this region. Newly independent states and deep-rooted hostilities among diverse religious and ethnic groups emerged. In 1948, with the establishment of the new state of Israel and the neighbouring Arab states' refusal to accept its existence, the instability of the region grew.

International attention focused on the unrest in the Middle East because of the region's oil and its proximity to the Soviet Union. The Arab-Israeli wars came the closest that any war had come to causing a confrontation between the United States and the Soviet Union.

On 14 May 1948, the United Nations declared the creation of the State of Israel, the British withdrew from Palestine, and several Arab states – Egypt, Transjordan, Lebanon, Iraq, and Saudi Arabia – attacked Israel. When the First Arab-Israel War ended in 1949, Israel emerged victorious. Since the foundation of Israel, the Israelis have had to face two threats: an internal one from Arab insurgents and from the 'hit-and-run' attacks by the Palestine Liberation Organization (PLO), and an external threat coming from the regular forces of the nation's Arab neighbours. Until the beginning of the Palestinian *intifada* (uprising) in 1987, the latter was by far the more serious. Between 1948 and 1956, the state of Israel created for itself an effective military force.

Prior to the annexations of territory captured in 1967, Israel's major strategic problems included vulnerable frontiers and economic and demographic weaknesses. Israel, because of its size, could not risk a war of linear or elastic defence or of prolonged attritional struggle. In addition, Israel could not afford to maintain a large standing army. Consequently, the Israelis developed a concept of the 'nation in arms'. The Israeli Defence Forces (IDF) consisted of a small professional component and a large citizen militia. Employing universal conscription of men and women, the Israelis created a reserve force that could be mobilized in 72 hours. In the event of an enemy attack, the regulars' role was to 'hold the ring' until the reserve forces could be mobilized.

ISRAELI MOBILITY

Armour and tactical air power provided the basis for the IDF's striking power. Between 1948 and 1956, the IDF relied on light armour and mechanized infantry instead of tanks. In the 1956 war with Egypt, the Israelis implemented a pre-emptive *Blitzkrieg* in their crushing victory. Following their success, the Israelis modernized and strengthened the IAF (Israeli Armoured Forces). They placed greater emphasis on the tank, which had proven successful in the campaign. Moshe Dayan became an enthusiastic convert. By 1967 tank extremists claimed that tanks could win

battles on their own. Israel's scarce resources purchased tanks rather than artillery or armoured personnel carriers. By 1967 Egypt and Syria had equipped their forces with Soviet kit and trained them in Soviet 'sword and shield' tactics. 'Shields' of infantry, minefields, antitank weapons and armour would hold enemy attacks while armoured/mechanized formations launched counterattacks.

In 1967 the fragile peace that existed in the Middle East ended. Although a United Nations force patrolled the border of Israel on the Sinai and the Gaza Strip, the border with Syria and Jordan was characterized by ambushes, attacks on civilians, and frequent reprisals. In early May, Nasser learned from the Soviets about the Israelis' preparations for an attack against Syria. Although the information later proved to be incorrect, Nasser mobilized his reserves and moved units into the Sinai. Nasser persuaded the United Nations to remove its forces from the Sinai. Egyptian forces occupied the strategic position at the mouth of the Gulf of Aqaba – Sharm el-Sheikh – and cut off Israeli shipping through the Gulf. The Egyptian actions started the Six-Day Arab-Israeli War of 1967.

BELOW: On a routine border patrol, scouts from the Berlin Brigade's Combat Support Company (CSC), drawn from the 4th Battalion, 6th US Infantry Division, check on activity on the Communist side of the Berlin Wall.

Because they realized that they would have to work together to defeat Israel, the Arabs established a unity of command. An Egyptian general commanded the Arab forces on the Jordanian front. The Egyptians also commanded an Iraqi force. Troops from Kuwait and Algeria helped the Arab forces surround Israel. The combined Arab forces outnumbered the Israelis almost two to one. The Arabs had three times as many tanks and almost three times as many aircraft. Because of the diversity of the Arab forces, however, it was inconceivable that there could be any true unity of command.

The Israelis, having learned of the impending attack, quietly mobilized their reserves, and then implemented a pre-emptive air strike on 5 June. Withing the first few hours of the war, the Israelis' crippled the Arabs' air power. Of the 418 Arab aircraft destroyed during the war, almost 300 were lost on the first day. Once the Israelis controlled the skies, the IAF could decisively influence the conduct of the ground war. Their central position would allow the Israelis to move their forces from one front to another. The first stage of the ground campaign began on 5 June when an Israeli armoured division attacked along the coast in the northern part of the Sinai

and captured Bir Gifgafa. Three Israeli divisions engaged and virtually destroyed two Egyptian 'shields' and one 'sword'. Over the next three days, the Israeli divisions exploited their success. By 8 June, advance Israeli forces reached the Suez Canal and exchanged antitank and artillery fire with the Egyptians on the other side of the canal. The IDF succeeded in destroying the Egyptian forces and clearing the Sinai Peninsula.

Jordan entered the battle on the central front around noon on 5 June. Following an artillery barrage, a small Jordanian force crossed the border south of Jerusalem. In response, the Israelis captured Jerusalem and isolated the high ground north of the city that runs parallel to the Jordan River valley. Following attacks on the north and south ends of the high ground, the Israelis controlled all the bridges over the river. Cut off, the Jordanians had no hope of victory. Although the Jordanian forces fought well, the IAF's armour, infantry, and air power overwhelmed them.

The Israelis turned next to the Syrians who had been relatively quiet during the first few days of the war. Early on 9 June, after launching heavy air strikes, the Israeli ground forces attacked. On the Golan Heights, the terrain made Syrian sword and shield defences even more

BELOW: The Israeli Army has seen more combat than most over the last half century, and it trains constantly to keep its edge. Here a field commander with the elite Golani Brigade establishes contact with headquarters during manoeuvres.

formidable. By the end of the first day, however, the Israelis controlled the forward slope of the northern Golan Heights. The next morning, Israeli troops forced their way through the defenders. An Israeli armoured division broke through in the south while paratrooopers hit the Syrians' rear positions. At 18:30 hours on 10 June, a United Nations ceasefire began as resistance by the Syrians fell apart. Although the Syrians held out for 36 hours, the combined use of armour and tactical air power enabled the IDF to achieve victory.

SIX-DAY WAR

The Six-Day War in 1967 was a remarkable victory for Israel. The IDF's use of pre-emptive air strikes against the enemy's air forces, followed by armour-led *Blitzkrieg* supported by tactical air power, proved devastating. The IDF had modified and improved the German version of *Blitzkrieg*. Unlike the Germans, however, the Israelis did not permanently eliminate the Arab threat. The war increased the presence of the United States and the Soviet Union in the Middle East. Although Israel had won the war, the Arabs refused to acknowledge the loss of territory. They demanded the return of the Sinai and the Golan Heights.

For the next three years, the Egyptians would engage in a 'War of Attrition,' in which they launched attacks – cross-border raids, artillery barrages, and air strikes – against positions held by the IDF, who engaged in retaliatory commando raids. Israel, supported by the United States, demanded a negotiated peace settlement in exchange for the occupied territories, as well as an increase in arms shipments to Israel. The Soviets, who consented to rearm Israel and Syria, began sending arms directly to the Arab nations instead of through another country, such as Czechoslovakia. Uprooted Arabs formed the PLO and engaged in terrorist activities against the Israelis. In August 1970, tired of the situation, the Arabs and Israelis agreed to another ceasefire.

Israel's successes in 1967 resulted in a bigger push for 'all-tank' theories. By 1973 the 'tank-heavy' armoured brigades placed less emphasis on all-arms cooperation. The 'armoured shock' of the frontal assault received the most focus. The available resources purchased tanks and aircraft, not APCs and artillery. The IDF built fixed defences in the Sinai and the Golan Heights. These defences, along with air strikes and mobile defences, were supposed to absorb an initial enemy attack. Recognizing the IDF's superiority in mobile warfare in 1967, the Egyptians planned a limited campaign. They would move into the Sinai and then go on the defence. They would basically invite the IDF to attack. The superior Egyptian numbers and firepower would overcome the superior skill of the IDF. Soviet-supplied antitank and antiair missiles would provide the firepower. At that

point, the Egyptians hoped that the United States along with the Soviet Union would step in and negotiate a compromise peace. This peace, they hoped, would fall in favour the Arab states in the area.

Following Nasser's death in 1970, the more moderate Anwar Sadat became the president of Egypt. Although he did not want to decisively defeat the Israelis, Sadat decided to go to war in October 1973. Believing that a limited victory would result in political gains, Sadat persuaded Syria and Jordan to join the fight so that the Israelis would have to fight a two-front war. Before going to war, Sadat obtained sophisticated weapons from the Soviets and improved the readiness of his forces. Unlike 1967,

ABOVE: The aerial threat remains as dangerous today as it was at the end of World War II. However, the development of sophisticated man-portable surface-to-air missiles like the Short Starstreak (two versions of which are shown here) has given the foot soldier more firepower when confronted by attack helicopters or ground-attack aircraft.

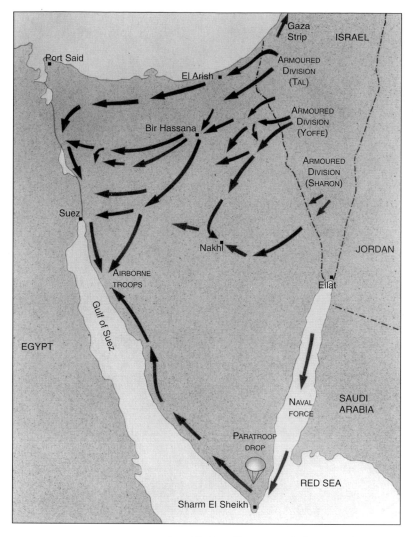

series of coordinated blows. With these actions, they forced the IDF to defend two fronts at the same time as they were mobilizing. As a result, the Arabs briefly threatened to defeat Israel.

During the first three days of the war, attacks by the IDF resulted in heavy losses, because most of the IAF had been deployed to the Golan Heights and they had launched a series of unsupported frontal tank attacks. By 10 October, however, the IDF's situation gradually began to change.

On Sunday, 14 October, the Egyptians advanced out of their bridgeheads in six major thrusts, but the cost of their action was high. In the battle that resulted, about 2000 tanks participated. Although the Egyptian forces advanced over 15km (9.3 miles), they lost a total of over 260 tanks, while the IDF only lost 20. By implementing six thrusts, the Egyptians seriously weakened their offensive. The Israeli Air Force inflicted heavy losses. In addition, the IDF had been issued with a new weapon – the TOW (tube launched, optically tracked, wire-guided) antitank missile – and it was supplied by the United States.

CROSSING THE SUEZ CANAL

At 17:00 hours on 15 October, the Israelis moved on the Suez Canal. Fierce opposition failed to prevent one division from getting across and creating havoc among the surprised Egyptian divisions. Advance units of another two Israeli divisions crossed and destroyed the Egyptian's West Bank air defence sites, which allowed the Israeli Air Force to become more effective. The arrival of the IAF contributed to the IDF's recovery and re-established the balanced 'all-arms' formations that had fought so effectively a few years earlier.

The situation in the north, however, was very different. The Golan Heights was the scene of some of the most critical fighting because the Syrians posed a direct threat to Israel proper. Initially, two infantry divisions, reinforced by two tank battalions, defended the Heights. In late September the arrival of another armoured brigade increased the number of tanks to 175. On 6 October the Syrians attacked with three mechanized and two armoured divisions, which were supported by 32

ABOVE: During the 1967 Six-Day War, the Israelis launched a combined-arms air, tank and mobile infantry attack on Egyptian forces in the Sinai desert, prevailing over their more numerous opponents through a classic *Blitzkrieg* series of manoeuvres.

Israeli intelligence did not alert the nation about an impending attack. Consequently, the Arabs succeeded in surprising their enemy.

At 14:00 hours on 6 October 1973, which was the Jewish Sabbath and Yom Kippur, Egyptian and Syrian forces attacked and achieved surprise. While Egyptian forces struck along the entire canal front, the Syrians hit the Golan Heights. Air strikes and a huge artillery barrage prepared the way for five infantry divisions to cross the canal on rubber assault boats. The Egyptians used 50 SAM batteries (SA-6, SA-2, and SA-3) plus conventional cannon and man-portable SA-7 to support the infantry. Once across the canal, Egyptians dug in and waited for the Israelis to attack. By 20:00 hours, the Egyptians had managed to establish several bridgeheads. Egyptian antitank defences included their B-10 and B-11 recoilless guns, AT-3 ('Sagger') and RPG-7s, plus their tanks and various assault guns. The Arabs struck first, with a

SAM batteries and antitank missiles. The Syrian force included approximately 1500 tanks. Non-stop fighting lasted for three days and two nights. Superior tank gunnery and IAF support enabled the defenders to survive the first two days of fierce fighting. The arrival of reserves enabled the IDF to switch to the offensive for a two days between the 8th and the 10th of October.

By 10 October, the Israelis had forced the Syrians to retreat behind the 1967-truce line. The Israeli advance continued unchecked for almost two weeks before the United States and the Soviet Union finally urged an end to the conflict. The Soviets agreed to an international peacekeeping force as long as it did not include Soviet or American troops. The Israelis reluctantly agreed to a cessation of hostilities before the intervention of the international peacekeeping force. When the ceasefire began on 24 October the Israelis were not far from Damascus.

Israel had won, despite its being outnumbered. The success of the Israeli *Blitzkrieg* reinforced its importance, but the 'all-tank approach' had been discredited. Although Israel ultimately emerged victorious, Sadat's desire to demonstrate the vulnerability of the Jewish state also succeeded. Despite their losses, the Arabs had achieved a psychological victory over the Israelis.

In the midst of the Cold War, a series of wars occurred in the Middle East, and they were conducted without direct involvement of the United States or the Soviet Union, and without the use of nuclear weapons. The Israelis used conventional forces and conventional weapons to achieve victory, despite the fact that they were greatly outnumbered. During this same period, the United States and the Soviet Union developed military doctrines which were based on nuclear weapons. These doctrines would be put to the test in Southeast Asia; first in Korea, then in Vietnam.

ABOVE: Israel conducted manoeuvres in March 1967 in preparation for the Six-Day War. Although a sandstorm prevented Prime Minister Levi Eshkol from attending, the Army went ahead with a three-day exercise in the Negev desert.

BELOW: The 1967 Jerusalem Battle. Israeli and Arab forces engage in street fighting as each struggle for control of the Holy City.

CHAPTER EIGHT

PROXY WARS

Thankfully, the Cold War never turned hot. However, tension between the superpowers had to find an outlet, which usually took the form of proxy battles between Eastern and Western-influenced movements across the globe.

In the increasingly polarized world of the Cold War, there existed certainties of military thought that most western planners took for granted. The coming conflict between freedom and Communism would take place in western Europe, thus reducing the importance of and interest in other volatile areas of the globe. The war, when it came, would be massive – truly a Third World War – and would quite possibly involve the use of nuclear weapons and cause a global catastrophe. The future seemed quite bleak. The Soviet Union would attempt to expand. The United States would respond in an effort to contain that expansion, and the entire world would pay the price. It was in this atmosphere of 'mutually assured destruction' that both world superpowers began to place checks on their use of military force in attempts to stop the conflicts of the Cold War era from escalating towards totality. Thus the doctrine of Limited Warfare was born, in which the world superpowers would face off on battlefields across the globe, often fighting their murderous conflicts by proxy.

In the wake of World War II the United States, holding to past precedent, had rapidly de-mobilized its ground forces, choosing to rely on the nuclear deterrent and strategic air power in support of

LEFT: During 1950 infantrymen of the US 1st Infantry Division, armed with M-1 Garand rifles, search ruined Korean buildings for Communist infiltrators. The Korean 'Police Action' served as a template for Cold War proxy battles, differing only in the size and scale of the forces involved on both sides.

119

ABOVE: Communist forces advance in the wake of an artillery barrage in the Korean War. Both the initial assault by North Korean troops and the subsequent Chinese intervention in the conflict took US commanders by surprise.

efforts to contain Communist expansion. In the spring of 1950 there were only 10 active duty army divisions and 11 separate brigades available to respond to a military crisis. At the same time President Truman and his military advisers came to the conclusion that the nuclear deterrent was inherently dangerous and not sufficient to contain all Soviet expansion. In a document entitled NSC 68, the Truman presidency outlined the need for the capacity to meet the Soviet Union in limited war anywhere in the world, resulting in a renewed emphasis on traditional ground forces. Thus the decision had been made to meet Communist threats with military responses of equal intensity.

At the close of World War II, US and Soviet troops had entered Korea to disarm Japanese forces in the area. As the Cold War deepened, the dividing line between US and Soviet forces, at the 38th Parallel, hardened into a tense, international border between North and South Korea. Sidetracked by events in Europe the Americans remained unaware of a North Korean military build-up, and of preparations to invade South Korea. For their part, the Soviets misread US intentions in the area, believing that the Americans had written off South Korea and would not go to war for its

protection. On 23 June 1950 North Korean forces, numbering some 135,000 men, invaded South Korea, which was defended by an army of only 65,000. Facing little effective resistance, the North Koreans quickly seized Seoul and began the process of driving their defeated opponents into the sea.

Determined to save South Korea and contain Communist expansion, Truman turned to the United Nations. The UN Security Council, being boycotted by the Soviets at the time, approved a US-sponsored resolution giving the UN the mandate to defend South Korea from the unprovoked violation of its sovereignty. Control of the war in Korea fell to the United States, but forces from several UN member nations would take part in the fighting. Truman turned to General Douglas MacArthur to command US and UN forces in the conflict. At first the situation looked quite bleak for MacArthur, who could only rely on four understrength American infantry divisions located in Japan. Determined to achieve victory, MacArthur planned to construct a defensive perimeter around and hold firm at the port city of Pusan, while rushing US forces to the front in an effort to delay the North Korean advance. Elements of the 24th and 25th Infantry Divisions, though they were greatly outnumbered, succeeded in slowing the North Koreans, thus gaining valuable time for defensive preparations in the 'Pusan Perimeter'.

By early August the North Koreans had begun attacks on the UN defensive enclave, still holding a numerical advantage over the Eighth Army. Often utilizing human-wave tactics, the North Koreans sorely pressed the US and South Korean defenders. Though the situation was dire, MacArthur held much-needed reinforcements in reserve, waiting to launch an amphibious operation designed to alter the entire war. On 15 September, X Corps, under the command of General Edward Almond, executed a daring amphibious landing in very difficult tidal conditions at Inchon. Though fighting in the area, especially around Seoul, was furious, on 23 September when threatened with envelopment, the North Koreans began a general withdrawal. Aided by punishing air strikes, UN forces quickly drove into North Korea, nearing a complete victory. Truman, though, remained quite conscious that the presence of US forces

along the Yalu River might prompt a formal Chinese entrance into the conflict, an unwelcome escalation towards a true superpower clash. Though steps were taken to placate the Chinese, US military advisers underestimated their reaction to developments in Korea. On 25 November a Chinese force numbering nearly 200,000 men slammed into the exhausted Eighth Army, forcing a hasty UN retreat. Though US air power took a great toll on the Chinese attackers, US and UN forces withdrew to a point below the 38th Parallel and once again Seoul fell to Communist control.

The war in Korea had now become a direct conflict between forces of the United States and China, a situation that rapidly could escalate into a general world conflict. Realizing that the situation had changed dramatically, MacArthur sought more troops and supplies and a new level of national commitment to make war on a much more powerful opponent. For complete victory in Korea the war would have to be taken to China. The Truman government, though, wanted no part of

BELOW: Marines using scaling ladders during the landing at Inchon. The difficult tidal conditions in the area made the amphibious operation perilous, but that also meant that it came as a surprise to the North Koreans who occupied Seoul.

ABOVE: Troops of 3rd Battalion, Royal Australian Regiment, lay down covering fire during operations in Korea. Many battles of the Cold War would have a multi-national component, or were fought entirely by proxy forces.

an all-out war with China. Such a conflict would certainly lead to a clash with the Soviet Union and general war in Europe. Truman instead opted for a more limited war of strategic defence of South Korea. MacArthur bristled at the notion of fighting a war designed to result in a draw, a war that never brought military force to bear on the real enemy: China. By April 1951 differences between Truman and MacArthur had come to a head, resulting in MacArthur's dismissal. The goals of the war and the force used to prosecute the war would

remain limited. Neither the western Allies nor the Soviet bloc desired escalation in Korea; the possible catastrophic results were simply not worth the risk. Thus from 1951 onwards neither side fought for victory and the reunification of Korea. Neither side, though, would accept defeat, and the war in Korea dragged on, developing into a stalemate around the 38th Parallel.

As peace negotiations slowly moved forward, the combatants did battle in prepared defensive emplacements attempting to improve their negotiating position. Thus the war became a trench war aimed at very limited goals, goals more of a diplomatic nature than a military nature. Chinese forces relied on their strength in numbers, sending human waves into attacks that more closely resembled the Somme than battles from World War II. US and UN forces relied on superior defensive firepower and constant air attacks on the Communists' logistic system. Through the tireless efforts of nearly 500,000 labourers, though, the Communist supply lines remained open and effective. The rather primitive Communist logistic network actually proved a very poor target for a modern, technological bombing campaign, a case which would be repeated in the war in Vietnam.

On 27 July 1953 the Korean War ended in a negotiated armistice, ending in many ways where it had begun, along the 38th Parallel. The first major conflict of the Cold War set the rules of modern, limited warfare. US forces had defended South Korea from defeat, thus upholding the doctrine of 'containment'. The amount of force used in Korea had been only enough to stem defeat, avoiding escalation and sublimating the desire for conflict with the real enemy: worldwide Communism. The North Koreans had been denied their goal of conquering South Korea but Chinese forces had at least defended their client state from destruction. Utilizing strength in numbers, the Chinese had prolonged the war long enough to gain what they considered to be an honourable settlement. The parameters of limited warfare had been established, and most military pundits believed that the next limited war which involved the world superpowers would closely resemble the conflict in Korea.

MALAYA AND COUNTERINSURGENCY

Many struggles of the Cold War era were less formal than the Korean War in nature, often taking the form of Communist-inspired insurgencies against governments supported by the western Allies. Insurgent forces, disaffected members of the populace, usually relied on guerrilla warfare and terrorism in their struggles, and often followed the military template set by the Communist revolution in China. Mao Tse-tung had utilized a pattern of protracted war and by 1949 had overthrown the Nationalist régime of Chiang Kai-shek. Using time to create will, the Chinese insurgents had melted into the countryside to indoctrinate the great masses of people in the ideals of revolution.

Fending off government attacks and utilizing guerrilla tactics, the Maoist forces slowly gained adherents while keeping constant pressure on government forces in a slow war of attrition. Time was all-important to the insurgent. In a war that could last for several decades the capitalist government, unwilling and unable to make the necessary concessions to win the true support of the people, would eventually succumb to defeat. Maoist protracted warfare was a recipe for the weak to defeat the strong. Gradually, over a time, the tiny bites would have a cumulative effect and the mosquito would finally defeat the elephant.

During World War II the latent Malayan Communist Party (MCP) had become an armed force standing against Japanese rule. After the close of the conflict the forces of the MCP, led by the charismatic Chin Peng, launched an insurgency designed to overthrow British rule and convert the state to communism. At first glance Malaya seemed to be an ideal place to implicate Maoist protracted war. Covered in dense jungle, the terrain offered the insurgents ample cover. In addition, the insurgents found welcome support from amongst an impoverished Chinese minority population.

The MCP did, however, face several disadvantages in its insurgent campaign. The insurgents, only numbering some 8000 fighters, received little in the way of outside support, and in many ways their message of revolt carried little weight outside the Chinese community. Most Malays remained quite content to live under a rather benign form of British colonialism and were unwilling to risk their lives, realizing that British rule would soon come to a voluntary end. The insurgents often seemed more like thugs than champions of the people, routinely resorting to terrorism and brutality to keep their supporters in line.

OPPOSITE: US Marines engage in house-to-house fighting after the Inchon landings. The surprise of the landings swung the fortunes of war in favour of the UN forces.

BELOW: SAS men in Malaya prepare for a combat jump against Communist guerrillas. Using the experience of the Chindits as a guide, the SAS would set many of the standards for successful counterinsurgency warfare.

Continuing guerrilla raids and terrorist attacks in 1948 forced the British to declare a state of emergency in Malaya. Soon the British had sent a force equalling the strength of two divisions to Malaya to root out the insurgent force. Working in an uneasy and ineffective alliance with the colonial police force the British relied on sizeable military sweeps designed to corner and crush the insurgent fighting forces. However, British intelligence was poor and their enemy was quite elusive, with the result that most of the sweeps met with very little success. At the same time guerrilla activities in Malaya consistently increased. The British, it seemed, were now losing the war.

HEARTS AND MINDS

In 1951 there were some 600 guerrilla attacks throughout Malaya. General Sir Harold Briggs, the new British military commander in the area, though, had developed a plan for victory. The war in Malaya was political in nature and required a political solution. The Briggs Plan called for cooperation between civil and military authorities, designed to separate the insurgents from their base of support. In a 'hearts and minds' campaign of reforms and education, the British colonial authority capitalized on the support of the majority of the Malayan population. The British even promised the Malays independence by 1957, thus crippling any claim the MCP had to being the leaders of a nationalist rebellion. Possibly of the greatest importance, though, the Briggs Plan called for the resettlement of the Chinese squatter population. Construction began on new villages for the Chinese and they were promised farmland and a cash allowance. Most of the Chinese were only too happy to leave the squatter camps behind to benefit from a better life in the new villages. The new British plan severed the MCP from the population, thus denying the insurgents cover, succour and new conscripts.

Though the political aspects of counterinsurgency in many ways took precedence, the British also altered their military philosophy in Malaya. Once isolated from the people, the insurgents were quite vulnerable to attack. The British chose to scrap lumbering sweeps

by large units through the jungle in search of their elusive prey. Utilizing superior intelligence gained from supportive locals and MCP defectors, British forces prepared to make use of jungle warfare tactics of the past to bring the conflict to a conclusion. Ex-Chindit Michael Calvert had raised and helped train a special jungle warfare unit of the Special Air Service (SAS). Founded in World War II, the SAS had specialized in sabotage and commando raids, and was the forerunner of modern special forces units. After undergoing extensive training in jungle warfare, the unit – designated the Malayan Scouts – deployed to a series of forts along the fringes of the massive jungle that served as the MCP sanctuary.

The SAS forces led long-range penetration patrols in the best traditions of the Chindits. Utilizing stealth and speed the SAS would drive deep into the jungle – with little in the way of supplies or support – and live off of the land in search of their beleaguered foe. Limiting their use of firepower to minimize collateral damage, the SAS kept the MCP insurgents on the run and

consistently guessing. In some ways the SAS employed guerrilla tactics in fighting the guerrillas. The results were quite successful and led to a collapse of the insurgency. As promised Malaya received its independence in 1957, and by 1960 the stage of emergency within the country had finally ended.

British success in Malaya served as the template for future counterinsurgency campaigns during the Cold War era. Continuing insurgent conflicts from Cuba to Africa would play a key role in the ongoing superpower struggle, becoming much more common than limited war. Western nations often saw insurgencies as only military in nature, requiring a military solution. Though sometimes successful, purely military solutions to insurgency often resulted in disaster. In Malaya the British had recognized that separation of the insurgent from the population through political means was paramount, as it allowed for an eventual military victory utilizing tactics of irregular warfare. In subsequent wars, notably in Vietnam and Afghanistan, counterinsurgency methods

OPPOSITE TOP: British troops practise battlefield insertion from a Whirlwind Mark 10 helicopter in 1965. The speed with which they could deploy troops into difficult terrain would make the helicopter a mainstay of counterinsurgency campaigns around the globe.

OPPOSITE BOTTOM: British troops of the 22nd SAS Regiment patrol the Temenggon area of Northern Malaya in 1954. Innovative SAS tactics coupled with an effective 'hearts and minds' campaign proved to be a war-winning combination in Malaya (now Malaysia).

LEFT: A Wessex helicopter of the Royal Navy delivers Gurkhas to an improvised border landing zone during the confrontation with Indonesia over Borneo.

ABOVE: The French relied on firepower and mobility including combat air assaults in an effort to bring the elusive Viet Minh to battle. Here, the beleaguered garrison at Dien Bien Phu is reinforced from the air.

would sometimes be applied but would often be overlooked or undervalued as both the United States and the Soviet Union emphasized the lessons of conventional limited war.

THE FAILURE OF LIMITED WAR

Though the wars in Korea and Malaya were dissimilar and, in the main, unrelated, the Cold War policy-makers of the United States thought quite differently. Communism was viewed as a monolithic entity, controlled from Moscow, and an entity bent on world domination. Communists in Korea and Malaya – taking part in limited war or revolution – were regarded as but a part of a greater conspiracy against the West. Thus the US considered the Cold War to be a vast, global conflict involving interlocking wars of several types, wars which were directed by the Soviet Union. It was President Truman who gave voice to the evolving policy of the US in the face of what he viewed as Soviet expansionism by stating that the United States would 'assist all free peoples against threats of revolution and attack from without'.

After World War II the French sought to re-assert their authority over Vietnam, which had fallen to the rule of the Japanese. However, the Viet Minh – under the charismatic leadership of Ho Chi Minh – rose up against French rule, sparking a war that would last for nearly 30 years. The Vietnamese insurgents, undersupplied and numbering only 60,000, faced long odds against 200,000 well-armed and highly motivated French troops. Realizing his weakness Ho decided to avoid battle, relying on the attrition of Maoist protracted war to achieve victory and declaring to his French adversaries, 'If we must fight we will fight. You will kill ten of our men and we will kill one of yours. Yet it is you who will tire first.' Unlike the insurgents in Malaya, the Viet Minh enjoyed wide national support in their struggle. Unwilling to reform and unable to offer independence, the French authorities did little to solve the political problems that foment revolution. Thus Ho Chi Minh was able to stand more as a true Nationalist leader rather than a Communist revolutionary. Because the French had done little to win the 'hearts and minds' of the Vietnamese, the Viet Minh insurgency grew in strength, eventually garnering considerable aid and military support from both the Soviet Union and China.

As the conflict in Vietnam became more serious it attracted the notice of the United States. In 1949 the French divided Vietnam in half near the 17th Parallel, proclaiming South Vietnam to be 'free'. The cunning diplomatic move allowed the French to present their colonial war in Vietnam in stark Cold War terminology. South Vietnam – actually a French colonial construct that never requested or desired statehood – was a small nation beset by Communist revolution and invasion. Ho Chi Minh's nationalist uprising was but a well-concealed part of the global Communist conspiracy. South Vietnam was, then, very like South Korea, and could not be allowed to fall, lest 'containment' fail. Indicating new levels of US commitment to the war in Vietnam, in his 1952 inaugural address President Eisenhower remarked, 'the French in Vietnam are fighting the same war we are in Korea'.

By 1954 French national support for the conflict in Vietnam had waned, and French rule in Vietnam came to a disastrous end at the Battle of Dien Bien Phu. Unwilling to see containment fail in Southeast Asia, the United States used diplomacy and threats to assure the continued survival of South Vietnam in the Geneva Accords. Realizing, though, that the war was far from over and that Ho Chi Minh would seek to reunify his country, the United States soon began to send aid as well as advisers to South Vietnam, in the hopes that they could build a nation where none existed.

The South Vietnamese régime, though, was singularly uncooperative. Though it professed to be a democracy South Vietnam was a brutal dictatorship, one that was shot through with graft and inefficiency. The régime had little to offer its people other than poverty and repression, helping the Viet Minh – now called the Viet Cong (VC) – insurgency to grow. By 1965 the Communist insurgents controlled over 60 per cent of the land area of South Vietnam, and the CIA estimated that in a free election

BELOW: French and loyal Vietnamese forces on patrol on 2 February 1954 outside Dien Bien Phu. Such patrols failed to detect a Viet Minh build-up in the area, which led to the later catastrophic French defeat, effectively ending French colonial rule in Vietnam.

some 80 per cent of the population would choose to follow Ho Chi Minh. The US policy of nation-building in South Vietnam had failed, and the régime teetered on the brink of collapse. Seeing containment threatened yet again, the first US combat forces entered South Vietnam on 8 March 1965, confident in their abilities to destroy the insurgent force of a Third World country.

The United States chose to fight the Vietnam War as a limited conflict, seeking only to assure the survival of South Vietnam and the success of containment. As a result US forces would never, in a systematic way, invade North Vietnam or the neighbouring countries of Cambodia and Laos, which provided the Communists with safe base camps and logistic networks. In addition, President Johnson would never fully mobilize US military forces or the popular support of the American people, choosing instead to limit homefront

involvement in the conflict. Vietnam became a war that the United States fought with only a small portion of its military and national might, and a war aimed not at specific, obtainable victory but rather at the defence of a rather nebulous status quo. American military planners initially thought little of the difficulties inherent in such limitations, for the problem in Vietnam seemed quite simple. An armed insurgent force, with significant aid from North Vietnam and the Communist bloc, threatened the existence of South Vietnam. The United States military, the most powerful force on the planet, would simply hunt down and destroy the insurgents, putting an end to the problem. Thus most US military planners viewed Vietnam as a rather traditional conflict with a purely military solution, paying little heed to the political and social reasons for the insurgency. Though the US would spearhead a 'hearts and minds' campaign

BELOW: The personification of air mobility. US helicopters hit a landing zone near Bong Son as part of 'Operation Eagle's Claw' in 1966. Ferried into battle by helicopters, US and ARVN (South Vietnamese) forces could strike at Communist troop concentrations across the length and breadth of South Vietnam.

ABOVE: US advisers arrived in Vietnam in the early 1960s, and were soon fighting alongside their South Vietnamese students against the Communist Viet Cong guerrillas. Here, an adviser leads a Vietnamese patrol through the waterlogged Plain of Reeds, 64km (40 miles) from Saigon, in an operation which took place in 1962.

it always stood second to the military effort. Strategically, then, the US viewed Vietnam as another limited war, and chose to limit the application of force to such a degree as to make the war almost unwinnable. Tactically the US prepared to fight a traditional campaign, but this would be to the detriment of true techniques of counterinsurgency. Of course, the mixture was quite volatile.

COMMUNIST REALITY

Though the Americans in many ways fought the wrong war, the North Vietnamese leadership realized that a military showdown with the Americans would be suicidal. Early attempts at conventional battles would prove the point. In the Ia Drang Valley in 1965, substantial US forces clashed with and defeated Viet Cong and North Vietnamese Army (NVA) units for the first time. The battle would set the tactical precedent for the remainder of the conflict. General Vo Nguyen Giap once again chose to rely on Maoist protracted war to even the odds. In command of the American and Allied forces, General Westmoreland adhered to a policy of large unit operations designed to 'find, fix and finish' the enemy.

US forces relied on search-and-destroy missions to locate and neutralize their elusive enemy. Many such missions met with little success, while others led to clashes with Communist forces, usually entrenched and informed of American movements. By late 1956, Giap chose to seek battle against the Americans to get

the measure of his impressive new foe. An NVA build-up in the Central Highlands led to a Communist siege of a US Special Forces camp at Plei Me. Though the attack failed, NVA and VC forces lingered in the area of the Ia Drang Valley. To Westmoreland the situation was perfect. The enemy had been located and had not fled to the sanctuary of Cambodia. Relying on superior firepower, US forces would make the NVA and VC pay.

In the coming battle US forces would rely on their overpowering edge in firepower as a decisive force multiplier. With control of the air, US ground troops could rely on the support of a vast array of aircraft from AC-47 'Spooky' gunships that could pepper targets with 100 rounds per second, to the massive force of B-52 strategic bombers. On the ground US forces crisscrossed South Vietnam with artillery Fire Support Bases (FSBs). Ringed with powerful defences and often the subject of Communist attacks, the FSBs in many ways formed the backbone of the US military effort in Vietnam.

Artillery, usually batteries of 105mm and 155mm guns, would support any search-and-destroy operation in the immediate area. When engaged in combat, US forces would communicate target coordinates to the FSB, which would reply with a devastating barrage of fire. Thus the US hoped to capitalize on its overwhelming firepower edge, enabling even small US forces to pin the enemy into battle with impunity.

Fixing the enemy into battle remained the elusive part of the equation, but Westmoreland believed he had the answer. The helicopter had seen limited military use in Korea, but would be a tactical mainstay in Vietnam. Before 1965 insurgent forces had been able to strike and flee into impenetrable jungle terrain, sure in the knowledge that they could outmanoeuvre any clumsy attempts at pursuit. Aboard helicopters, though, US forces could respond almost instantly to any enemy threat across the length and breadth of South Vietnam, leaving the enemy with no safe haven.

In a tactic which was known as air mobility, US forces, often very small in numbers and reliant upon their firepower edge, would chopper into areas known as Landing Zones (LZ), which were usually chosen for their proximity to a suspected enemy troop concentration. Thus anywhere the enemy operated, the helicopters would soon arrive, carrying troops designed to lock the now located enemy into battle, while massive firepower support assured their destruction. The formula was relatively simple. The superior mobility afforded by helicopters would negate the guerrilla's traditional elusiveness. Denied their primary defence, the application of

ABOVE: Staff Sergeant Collier of the 173rd Airborne amid a burning Viet Cong base camp in War Zone C in 1967. Such search-and-destroy missions were a major part of the US strategy of attrition employed in Vietnam.

RIGHT: US reconnaissance troops leap from a Bell UH-1 'Huey' in a speedy exit over a mountaintop near a suspected Viet Cong base camp. With soldiers standing on the landing skids and leaping from about 19m (6ft) in altitude, 32 men could be landed from six helicopters in less than a minute.

massive firepower would quickly attrit insurgent forces in South Vietnam, leading to total victory.

YEARS OF ATTRITION

On 14 November 1965 the 1st Battalion, 7th Cavalry, commanded by Colonel Harold Moore, flew by helicopter to LZ X-Ray near the Chu Pong Massif in the Ia Drang Valley. Having landed amidst a major NVA staging area, Moore's forces immediately fell under heavy attack. Two NVA regiments, the 33rd and the 66th, attempted to surround and destroy the tiny American force which held a LZ no larger than a football pitch. In savage, often hand-to-hand fighting, the US force grimly held its ground, receiving little by air on the now deadly LZ.

As expected, during the struggle massive US firepower support made the critical difference. Withering artillery barrages and the first tactical use of B-52 strikes, each aircraft laden with 16,329kg (36,000lb) of high explosive, took a terrible toll on NVA and VC forces. After three days of fighting, bloody and beaten, the Communist forces made for their safe havens in Cambodia. In a tragic postscript to the battle, the 2nd Battalion, 7th Cavalry stumbled into a carefully planned Vietnamese ambush and was nearly destroyed while moving to nearby LZ Albany. Even after taking this into account, US forces won a substantial tactical victory in the Ia Drang Valley, losing some 305 dead. In contrast the Communists lost an estimated 3561 dead out of 6000.

Westmoreland seemed vindicated. Helicopter mobility had pinned the enemy into battle, and firepower had prevailed, and this resulted in a favourable rate of attrition of more than 11 to 1. Certainly a few more such successes would ensure victory – a military victory – leaving little reason to rely on the more political and social aspects of a counterinsurgency campaign. Since the military objective had been the destruction of the enemy force, once the NVA and VC fled the area, it no longer held any tactical value. American troops returned to their base camps to await their next opportunity to fix their opponents into battle. Vietnam, then, was not a war about taking and holding ground, rather it was a war about

finding and killing the enemy: attrition at its most basic. There would be no great victories for the public to watch on television, and no pins for anxious relatives to move on campaign maps. There would be only the rough solace of the 'body count' to signify victory. Westmoreland's idea of victory was difficult for the American public to understand. As the war dragged on while the body count never translated into strategic victory, public support for the war slowly began to wane.

The NVA and VC also took several lessons from the Ia Drang. With his forces bloodied by the brush with superior American weaponry, Giap chose to avoid further battle, instead placing an increased reliance on safe havens in Cambodia and Laos in the main beyond the reach of US firepower. In South Vietnam Communist forces would engage in carefully prepared, small unit actions against the Americans, usually taking heavy, but acceptable losses, while

ABOVE: During 1967 members of this US Navy SEAL pause after discovering a Viet Cong booby trap, a Punji Bed, or bed of stakes. The use of booby traps and mines forced American troops to slow their patrols and caused a constant stream of injuries that diverted valuable American resources and sapped American morale.

slowly attriting US strength and eroding American support for the conflict. The strategy closely mirrored the prediction that Ho Chi Minh had made to the French years earlier. Thus even though the Americans held the edge in tactical mobility with the helicopter, the Vietnamese retained the initiative in the war. It was the Communists who chose to fight, or to flee. Tactically, the Communists had learned to neutralize the American firepower edge by 'grabbing American belts'. In battle Communist forces attempted to get as close to American troops as possible, realizing that the Americans would not risk calling down firepower on their own troops. In the end, then, Westmoreland and Giap learned much the same thing from the Battle of the Ia Drang Valley.

Many more such encounters could be lethal to the Communist insurgency. Westmoreland attempted to repeat his success, while Giap chose to fight by different rules, attempting to avoid future disastrous battles of attrition.

ROLLING THUNDER

For the next two years, the Vietnam War progressed through a series of large unit operations designed to wear down enemy strength. At the same time a massive but ill-fated bombing campaign over North Vietnam, 'Operation Rolling Thunder', was intended to force Ho Chi Minh to drop his support of the southern insurgents. From the Mekong Delta to the Demilitarized Zone (DMZ) US forces sought to bring the elusive enemy to battle in operations such as 'Junction City', 'Hickory', and 'Attleboro'. Though the operations often differed in tactics and terrain type – from rice paddies to mountain rainforest – they followed a similar pattern.

US forces, on the ground or by helicopter, would sweep into an enemy area, hoping to attrit enemy forces and 'pacify' the area. The Viet Cong, increasingly augmented by NVA forces, especially near the DMZ, were often aware of the coming sweep and prepared accordingly. Small Communist forces would meet the US or ARVN sweep in prepared positions, before inflicting as much damage as possible and then retreating to safe havens in Cambodia and Laos. In the encounter battles – such as the fight for Hill 875 near Dak To in 1967 – US forces usually inflicted a rate of attrition of over 10 to 1, but failed to destroy Communist units, which would survive to protract the war ever further. Unless they perceived an advantage, the Communists would not stand and fight at all. In 1968 US forces initiated over 1 million sweeps – from multi-divisional search- and-destroy operations to small scout team missions – and only 1 per cent made significant contact with the enemy. Even then US forces often took heavy casualties from mines and booby traps left behind by their elusive foe.

Thus the attritional struggle in Vietnam dragged on, and Westmoreland remained confident that the US was wearing down the Vietnamese will to fight and nearing overall victory. Westmoreland still

BELOW: Viet Cong guerrillas construct defensive tunnel networks by hand in the deep jungle. Seeking shelter the Viet Cong embraced mother earth, constructing thousands of miles of intricate tunnels throughout South Vietnam. Some of the complexes were so extensive that they even contained entire hospitals.

LEFT: US Marines charge up Hill 881 near Khe Sanh. The siege of the Marine base at Khe Sanh could have been another Dien Bien Phu, but unlike the French, the Americans had the air power both to keep the base supplied and to mount round-the-clock operations against the North Vietnamese Army.

believed that the conflict fit traditional patterns of limited war, and always expected a prototypical Communist ground offensive like that waged by China in the Korean War. The attritional rate of 'body count' gave Westmoreland reason for optimism, for in 1968 alone over 100,000 VC and NVA forces perished in battle. However, during the same year over 300,000 Communist troops moved down the Ho Chi Minh Trail, indicating that though the numbers ran heavily in favour of the United States, the war of attrition would indeed be quite lengthy. Even as Westmoreland predicted quick victory for US force of arms, the VC and NVA were preparing for their greatest offensive of the war.

A CHANGING WAR

On the morning of 30 January 1968, during the celebration of the Tet Lunar New Year, Viet Cong forces attacked urban centres across South Vietnam, abandoning the policy of protracted war to seek a decisive military victory. The reasons for the tactical change on the part of the Communists remain quite cloudy. Many historians in the West believe that the level of attrition from 1965 to 1967 made North Vietnamese

leaders unsure of the inevitability of victory in a protracted conflict, forcing a major military gamble in 1968. Others, including General Giap, portray the Tet Offensive as an act of revolutionary war against the Americans. The Viet Cong, fully aware that they could not defeat US military might in a traditional sense, hoped that their audacious offensive would spark a general uprising throughout South Vietnam, thus forcing the Americans to quit the country in

BELOW: A North Vietnamese soldier on alert for an air attack. In the face of the most concentrated bombing in history, Communist forces fought on with a tenacity that surprised American military planners.

ABOVE: Soldiers of the 2nd Battalion, 327th Infantry, fire M-16 rifles and an M-60 machine gun at NVA regulars north of Phu Bai during 1968. The development of lightweight assault rifles like the M16, firing small-calibre ammunition, gave the ordinary infantryman the kind of firepower, fully automatic firepower, previously only available to machine gunners.

defeat. Communist hopes, however, were soon dashed. Though the Viet Cong had attacked sensitive sites across the country, including the American Embassy in Saigon, the South Vietnamese people did not rise up in revolutionary ardour. From Can Tho to Quang Tri City, the Viet Cong attack had taken US and South Vietnamese forces largely by surprise. However, the attack merely served to lock the Communist forces into deadly battle, as Westmoreland had long hoped.

Only in the old imperial capital city of Hue did the fighting linger for long. The struggle for the city involved urban fighting reminiscent of Stalingrad in World War II. US and ARVN soldiers, used to jungle warfare, had quickly to adapt to street-to-street and house-to-house fighting to clear out determined pockets of enemy resistance. Having lost their mobility advantage and with artillery nearly useless in close-quarter fighting, US forces resorted to an all out bombardment of the enemy-held part of the city. During a month of street fighting, much of Hue was destroyed, and 75 per cent of its population made homeless, but the city was saved.

Near the border with Laos the last chapter of the Tet Offensive took place as nearly 40,000 NVA soldiers laid siege a force of 6000 US Marines at Khe Sanh. NVA artillery struck the base with

regularity and ground forces attacked outlying Marine positions using human wave tactics. Cut off from ground communications, the Marines relied on air support for their supplies and their salvation. Having finally located the elusive enemy, Westmoreland unleashed 'Operation Niagara' in defence of the Marines at Khe Sanh.

Devastating B-52 strikes pounded enemy positions in a round-the-clock aerial offensive, killing an estimated 10,000 NVA soldiers. In all American air power dropped the equivalent of 10 Hiroshima-sized atomic bombs in the Khe Sanh area, thus forcing the NVA to call a halt to their siege after some 77 days. During the Tet Offensive the Communist forces had fought bravely, but they had succumbed to superior American firepower, resulting in a staggering loss of life. Of some 85,000 Communist forces involved in the Tet Offensive, nearly 58,000 of them died, a fatality rate of over 70 per cent.

The Tet Offensive was a comprehensive military disaster that nearly destroyed the Viet Cong as an effective fighting force. In full retreat, the remaining VC cadres fled to Cambodia and Laos, thereby abandoning control of much of the Vietnamese countryside. At the same time, though, it became clear that the Tet Offensive had caused a massive shift in

American public opinion concerning the war in Vietnam. Though the war had been controversial, most Americans had been willing to believe their government's claims that the war was nearly over, claims the Tet Offensive seemed to disprove. For many Americans it now seemed that the war in Vietnam would linger indefinitely while US military men and women continued to die for a country that seemingly did not appreciate their presence or their sacrifice. The Tet Offensive, coupled with societal turmoil on the home front, caused American public support for the Vietnam War to plummet, even as Westmoreland sensed victory.

After the Tet Offensive, the Vietnam War changed yet again. Communist forces became more and more reliant on the efforts of the NVA, serving to alter the insurgent nature of the war. In addition Communist forces once again relied on guerrilla tactics in an effort to recover from their massive losses. US forces, too, altered their tactical methods of warfare, especially after General Abrams succeeded Westmoreland in overall command of the war. Partly due to strict orders to avoid taking casualties Abrams put an end to massive search-and-destroy operations, relying instead on the less traditional tactics of counterinsurgency. Thus General Abrams

introduced his 'One War' strategy, which aimed to blend battlefield victories with increased efforts at pacification throughout South Vietnam. Smaller units would patrol the countryside – and work with villagers to ensure their safety – rather than attempting to seek out and destroy elusive enemy main force units. Also, US Special Forces, in tandem with the CIA, undertook efforts to 'neutralize'

LEFT: Amid the rubble of intense urban warfare US Marines stop for a cigarette break. The nearly continuous fighting left many soldiers with lingering psychological problems that often did not become manifest until long after the fighting was over.

BELOW: South Vietnamese Marines return fire during the Tet Offensive in Saigon. Though the surprise Communist attack on the heart of American power was a military failure for the Viet Cong, it did much to convince Americans on the homefront that the war was being run incorrectly.

TOP: South Vietnamese soldiers move into battle during the North Vietnamese offensive of 1972. Though some ARVNs fought well, others were less effective, and there was little hope for victory once American troops had withdrawn.

ABOVE: After quick victories across the country, in 1975 North Vietnamese troops nearing their ultimate goal rush across the tarmac at Tan Son Nhut air base outside Saigon.

the VC infrastructure in the 'Phoenix Program'. Relying on such irregular tactics as political assassinations, the Phoenix Program met with great success, capturing over 34,000 VC operatives and 'neutralizing' thousands more, and in the process, destroying the control which the Communists had until that point held over numerous villages.

Though US tactics in the Vietnam War had changed, these changes came too late to achieve success in the conflict. Unlike the British situation in Malaya, the South Vietnamese Government was unwilling to offer meaningful political or economic reform to accompany the newly effective American military efforts. In addition the North Vietnamese

and the Viet Cong retained the support of the Soviet Union and China, indicating that the conflict could drag on for an indeterminate length of time. With social anarchy at home, and tumbling economic fortunes, the American public increasingly turned against the war in Vietnam. The change in political fortunes was mirrored by a policy of gradual de-escalation of American involvement in the war, conducting a policy that President Nixon would call 'Vietnamization'.

Unwilling to admit defeat or to see the immediate failure of containment, US forces slowly withdrew from Vietnam. Although the North Vietnamese launched a failed ground offensive in 1972, one that was in the main defeated by massive US air strikes, the last American forces exited the war in early 1973 after signing an armistice with the North Vietnamese. Nixon and his supporters realized that the war in Vietnam would continue, and few rational observers were taken by surprise when South Vietnam fell in 1975. The only shock was the speed with which South Vietnam collapsed.

Thus the Vietnam War ended as a victory for the North Vietnamese and a defeat for the American policy of containment. American forces had won every major battle, but had lost the war.

The effects of the first ever American defeat still linger, colouring every subsequent American use of military force. Many blamed the loss on US politicians who had reigned in the power of the military. It seemed, then, that the policy of limited war was to blame, and that the military limitations which were necessary to avoid escalation had made the conflict totally unwinnable.

In addition, the US disaster in Vietnam brought tactics of counterinsurgency into question. It seemed that the British success in Malaya had been an exception born more out of fortunate circumstances than of tactical and systemic success. In the United States the barrage of questions concerning the nature of warfare and the future projection of national power was dubbed the 'Vietnam Syndrome'. The US military had fallen into disarray and disfavour, and though it remained the most powerful nation in the world, the United States questioned its power. In every coming conflict, from Grenada to Kosovo to the War on Terror, the question would now rage, would the new war become 'another Vietnam'?

In the final analysis, limited war has its place and can be effective, as demonstrated in the Falklands and in the Gulf War. However, limited wars prosecuted by and between world superpowers are quite different and are often protracted and inconclusive. In Vietnam the United States tried to fight a limited war on the Korean model, expecting a traditional conflict against a traditional foe. However, the conflict in Vietnam defied western traditions. It was part war of national liberation, part insurgency, part civil war and part Cold War. Even as US forces abandoned their attritional policies in favour of counterinsurgent tactics, the Vietnam War defied labels and controls.

With massive external support, the Vietnamese insurgents and the NVA were able to persevere in the face of tactics that had defeated guerrilla forces elsewhere. Thus in many ways the Vietnam War was a hybrid conflict, part limited war and part insurgency. It was also an integral part of the Cold War.

As such, some military thinkers now see the American effort in Vietnam as a success, even though the country 'fell to Communism'. The US effort succeeded very obviously in one of its major goals, for Vietnam did not escalate into a new world war. Also if seen as one battle of the ongoing Cold War, Vietnam can be seen as something like the Battle of the Somme: a costly setback, but possibly an attritional success, on the way to eventual victory, one which was finally achieved with the fall of the Berlin Wall.

BELOW: North Vietnamese troops fan out through a defeated Saigon, signalling ultimate victory in the Vietnam War. The American failure in Vietnam would eventually redefine the American way of war.

CHAPTER NINE

LIMITED CONFLICTS

The end of the Cold War and advances in technology altered the very nature of modern conflict. The infantryman had to be prepared to deploy anywhere in the world, ready to fight limited wars for limited objectives.

In the wake of the Vietnam War military theorists world-wide began to question the effectiveness of limited war in the modern world. After all, if the armed forces of the world's leading superpower had failed to achieve victory against a Third World opponent, how would the militaries of lesser nations fare against similar or even greater threats? The conflict in Vietnam, though, had been unique in many ways and as such only had limited applicability as a new paradigm of modern conflict. Indeed a series of limited wars fought across the globe during the 1980s served to alter military perceptions concerning warfare in general. By the 1990s the success of small, élite forces, utilizing wondrous military technologies provided by the microchip revolution, seemed to indicate that limited war would indeed be the way of the future. The era of total war and threatened total destruction appeared to be over, as a Revolution in Military Affairs transformed conflict and returned decisiveness to war.

The first of the new limited wars pitted the United Kingdom against Argentina over ownership of the Falkland Islands. While neither nation ranked as a world military power, nor expected a major conflict in the Falklands, the war there set important precedents and

LEFT: A Sikorsky UH-60 Blackhawk flies over the Saudi Arabian desert in 1990, during 'Operation Desert Shield'. 'Desert Shield' was to become 'Desert Storm', and the defeat of Saddam Hussein's Iraqi forces seemed to indicate that new technology made it possible to win a decisive victory again, after nearly a century.

was much more revealing than the US conflict in Vietnam. For many years, Argentina had disputed British claims to ownership of the Falklands (Las Islas Malvinas), which was only 600km (373 miles) off of the Argentine coast. On 2 April 1982 Argentine forces, based on the strength of a large conscript army, struck the islands and quickly overcame the resistance of the small Royal Marine garrison, and within months the Argentines had sent some 13,000 reinforcements to the area. Their regional strength made the Argentines confident that Britain, over 12,000km (7458 miles) away, would not contest the loss of its distant dependency. Under the leadership of Prime Minister Margaret Thatcher, though, the British chose to strike back, and thus both countries made ready for an unexpected and unplanned conflict.

Reflecting the reality of the Cold War world, the British armed forces had been considerably downsized. Reliant upon training and technology as force multipliers, the British military had focused much of its attention on continuing troubles in Northern Ireland and did not expect to become involved in a limited national conflict. In the main incapable of prosecuting a large-scale war against Argentina, British planners limited the war to a contest for possession of the

Falkland Islands themselves. Quickly the British cobbled together a sizable force, consisting of over 8000 men and 39 warships, including two aircraft carriers, with which to launch their counterstrike. In preparation for the coming war Britain proclaimed an exclusion zone around the Falklands and by early May began to launch air- and naval bombardments against the Argentine defenders. Later in the month the British task force arrived in the area and an ensuing air battle heralded the beginning of 'Operation Corporate'. The Argentines, using aircraft based on the mainland, were left with little time to linger over the battle area. In addition the most advanced Argentine aircraft, Super Etendards and Mirages, did not fare well against British Sea Harriers. Even so, though the use of advanced Exocet missiles, Argentine pilots sank six British ships during the conflict including the Atlantic Conveyor, demonstrating a British weakness in radar detection.

Though brave Argentine pilots continued their strikes, the British had, in the main, established air superiority over the Falklands and now made ready for their landings on the islands. After a diversionary assault the British 3rd Commando Brigade and two parachute battalions landed against little opposition near San Carlos and Port San Carlos on the island of East Falkland. After consolidating their positions, the 2nd Battalion of the Parachute Regiment on 28 May launched on overland attack on Darwin and Goose Green. Though the fighting was intense and the 2nd Parachute Battalion lost its commanding officer, Colonel H. Jones, the British force quickly subdued a defending force more than three times its own size. British losses in the fighting were substantial – with the 2nd Parachute Battalion losing 10 per cent of its fighting strength – as the fleet at sea continued to suffer debilitating losses to Argentine air attacks. The capture of Darwin and Goose Green, though, served as morale boosters for the British and a signal of coming difficulties for the Argentineans.

TOWARDS PORT STANLEY

Now more wary of British strength the Argentinean commander, General Mario Menendez, stood ready to defend Port Stanley with nearly 9000 men. Convinced that the British had little stomach for real battle, Menendez arrayed his troops into defensive lines in the rugged hills and hoped to prosecute the war to a draw. However, the morale of

the Argentine defenders – mostly unwilling conscripts – fell to a dangerous low. Undersupplied, poorly clothed and not believing the war to be worth their sacrifice the Argentinean soldiers, though numerous, stood little chance in the coming battles. Utilizing helicopters whenever possible British forces, now numbering two brigades, slogged their way across the rugged terrain of East Falkland toward their now reluctant foe.

On the night of 11 June, the British force, under the overall command of General Jeremy Moore, struck the first line of Argentinean defences. Though resistance was sharp in areas, the well-trained and equipped British infantry soon infiltrated and compromised the defensive positions. Just two nights later the British struck again, augmented by heavy artillery fire, long before the Argentineans thought they could be ready. Once again the British outmanoeuvred and outfought their dispirited Argentinean foes and quickly seized the remaining high ground dominating Port Stanley. At this point Argentinean morale utterly collapsed, leading General Menendez to sign a surrender document ending the short,

BELOW: Members of the Scots Guards and the SAS move towards a helicopter on Goat Ridge in the Falklands. The highly trained British professionals were more than a match for the numerous, but poorly motivated Argentine conscripts.

ABOVE: Heavily laden British soldiers are resupplied by helicopter outside Darwin on the Falkland Islands. Although air mobility was of great help in the campaign, it was the classic infantry virtue of being able to march far and fast, carrying heavy loads, which enabled British forces to sustain a rapid advance over rugged terrain.

but sometimes quite bitter, conflict on 14 June. Losses in the Falklands War were relatively light: 255 British soldiers died as compared to 1000 Argentine fatalities.

The British experience in the Falklands War seemed to revalidate the concept of limited war. With precious little planning the British had made quick work of the conflict, achieving all of their major goals. More importantly, though, the war seemed to prove the efficiency of small, but highly professional armies. Utilizing superior training and morale, the British had been able to overcome a large, outdated conscript force with relative ease. The British also had exhibited high levels of all-arms coordination while the Argentinean forces had struggled to communicate and act as one. Finally in the Falklands War the British possessed a marked technological edge over their Second World opponent. In short, then, the war in the Falklands indicated that the armies of the West would fare well in more traditional wars against conscript armies of much larger size.

In the United States President Ronald Reagan, elected in 1980, sought to rekindle the nation's faith in itself. In 1983 a small Cuban military force and

the outbreak of societal revolution threatened the security of the tiny Caribbean island of Grenada. Not only were the Cubans in the process of constructing a major air base on the island but the safety of hundreds of American medical students also seemed to be in jeopardy. Thus on very short notice Reagan ordered a military operation – dubbed 'Urgent Fury' – to rescue the American students and force the Cubans and their supporters from the island. Though the Cubans were the tangible enemy in many ways the American attack on Grenada was a battle against the legacy of Vietnam.

Initially US forces estimated that they would face some 10 enemy battalions in Grenada, comprising both Cubans and local revolutionary forces. Wildly overestimating enemy strength, the US gathered together a large – if somewhat poorly organized – attacking force that numbered over 6000 men including elements of the Special Forces, the Marines, the 75th Rangers and the 82nd Airborne. With very little time to plan the operation, US forces began to land on Grenada on 25 October 1983, only three days after Reagan's order. Special Forces spearheaded the US assault on Grenada, including operations by Delta Force, Navy Seals and Army Rangers. Suffering from the lack of tactical planning and knowledge, though, most of the Special Forces units failed to achieve their objectives. Only the Seals succeeded by seizing and guarding the British governor of the area and holding out against repeated counterattacks.

AIRBORNE AGAINST GRENADA

Quickly Marine forces and a combat jump by the 1st Battalion, 75th Rangers seized the major airfields on the island, most notably at Point Salines. Here the rangers fell under heavy defensive fire but held the airport and succeeded in rescuing several US medical students. Though the airport was not yet truly secure, elements of the 82nd Airborne soon arrived by plane to augment American strength. Later that day an additional Marine force made an amphibious landing near the major Grenadan city of St George's against little opposition. On 26 and 27 October US units spread out from Point Salines attacking towards St George's and brushing aside Cuban and local defenders thus seizing control of the entire island.

'Operation Urgent Fury' had been a success, securing for the United States a much-needed victory in a limited war. Though the success helped to restore the nation's faltering faith, the seemingly

simple operation had been beset by several problems. The performance of the Special Forces units had been spotty at best, calling their use into question, especially in the wake of their failure of a few years earlier to rescue the Iranian hostages. In addition, the combined US force had exhibited multiple command and control problems. Such failures, especially in the wake of the nearly seamless British success in the Falklands, could not be tolerated. The shortcomings of 'Urgent Fury', together with the greater failure of Vietnam, changes in the

ABOVE: A dug-in and ready for action Royal Marine mortar team prepares to open fire from the wet and windy slopes of Mount Kent during the Falklands War.

BELOW: The attack on Goose Green was the first chance that British Paras had to measure themselves and their strengths against their Argentine opponents.

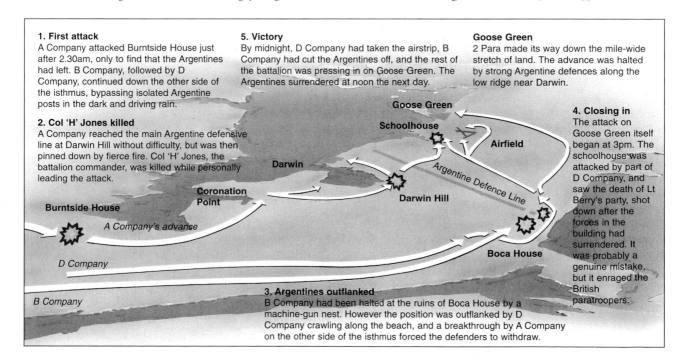

1. First attack
A Company attacked Burntside House just after 2.30am, only to find that the Argentines had left. B Company, followed by D Company, continued down the other side of the isthmus, bypassing isolated Argentine posts in the dark and driving rain.

2. Col 'H' Jones killed
A Company reached the main Argentine defensive line at Darwin Hill without difficulty, but was then pinned down by fierce fire. Col 'H' Jones, the battalion commander, was killed while personally leading the attack.

5. Victory
By midnight, D Company had taken the airstrip, B Company had cut the Argentines off, and the rest of the battalion was pressing in on Goose Green. The Argentines surrendered at noon the next day.

Goose Green
2 Para made its way down the mile-wide stretch of land. The advance was halted by strong Argentine defences along the low ridge near Darwin.

4. Closing in
The attack on Goose Green itself began at 3pm. The schoolhouse was attacked by part of D Company, and saw the death of Lt Berry's party, shot down after the forces in the building had surrendered. It was probably a genuine mistake, but it enraged the British paratroopers.

Goose Green
Schoolhouse
Airfield
Darwin
Argentine Defence Line
Coronation Point
Darwin Hill
Burntside House
A Company's advance
D Company
Boca House
B Company

3. Argentines outflanked
B Company had been halted at the ruins of Boca House by a machine-gun nest. However the position was outflanked by D Company crawling along the beach, and a breakthrough by A Company on the other side of the isthmus forced the defenders to withdraw.

ABOVE: A heavily armed American soldier scans a street in Grenville, Grenada during 'Operation Urgent Fury'. He is armed with an M-203 grenade launcher attached to an M-16A1 rifle and is also carrying an M-72 antitank rocket launcher.

nature of the Cold War and the advent of new technologies, led to a systematic redefinition of the American way of war in the mid-1980s and to what some called a Revolution in Military Affairs.

THE SOVIETS IN AFGHANISTAN

While the nations of the West engaged in victorious limited wars and began to redefine the nature of modern conflict the Soviet Union became bogged down in a war against guerrilla forces in Afghanistan. It was a war that closely resembled the US experience in Vietnam and a war that began the collapse of the massive Soviet empire. Fearing for the security of the pro-Soviet régime in their neighbour to the south, Soviet forces in December 1979 supported an Afghan coup. In tandem with a Special Forces operation in Kabul, four mechanized rifle divisions raced across the border to secure most of the major urban areas of the country and placed Babrak Karmal in power as President of the Democratic Republic of Afghanistan. The massive Soviet force quickly brushed aside resistance from loyal Afghan units and the war appeared to be at an end. Soviet military planners were quite confident that the Afghans – notoriously quarrelsome and ethnically divided – would put up only minor resistance to a

Soviet occupation force. The Soviet occupation, though, caused a great societal upheaval in Afghanistan, leading a total of five million refugees to flee the country. Backed by world opinion and fired by a religious fervour, Afghan rebels took to the rugged mountainous terrain of their nation's hinterland and called for a jihad, or holy war, against the infidel invaders. Though originally small in numbers the guerrillas, termed Mujahedeen, planned to protract their struggle, much as the Viet Cong had done in their war against the United States.

During the first phase of the conflict in Afghanistan, lasting nearly four years, the Soviets expected to crush the Mujahedeen using traditional military tactics dating from World War II and designed for the battlefields of western Europe. Increasingly the Soviet force, raised to a strength of 100,000 men, had to be self-reliant, as the army of their Afghan client government deserted to join the Mujahedeen at a stunning rate. The Mujahedeen for their part relied on traditional guerrilla hit-and-run tactics, launching lightning raids and ambushes on Soviet forces from their mountain hideaways. In addition the Mujahedeen could rely on safe bases of operations in and support from Iran and Pakistan. Like the United States in Vietnam, the Soviets dared not attack the Mujahedeen safe havens for fear of escalating the conflict. The war in Afghanistan, then, would be a limited war on the part of the Soviet Union, following many of the rules of failed efforts in previous such wars.

Initially Soviet military techniques in Afghanistan were clumsy and totally unsuited to the situation at hand. The Soviet theories of modern conflict revolve around their experience in World War II. Expecting any new war to be a total war in Europe, the Soviets were masters of massed armoured movements against an enemy expected to stand and give battle. Though their nation was an armed camp – in constant readiness for the expected massive land war – the Soviets had put little thought into conducting a war against elusive guerrillas, almost ignoring the western experiences of counterinsurgency and limited war. As they would in conflicts in Chechnya later, the Soviets simply attempted to defeat the Mujahedeen by

using the tactics and military doctrine that they had to hand. It was a mistaken attempt to attempt to alter the war rather than alter the fighting methods, a signal and eventually fatal flaw within the Soviet military system. Soviet and loyal Afghan forces, often of divisional strength, would use massive artillery and air support to prepare the battlefield. Following in the wake of the maelstrom, Soviet tanks and mechanized forces would lumber forwards into the countryside in vain attempts to locate and crush the guerrillas, who had already fled to their safe havens. Since much of the Soviet armour and mechanized infantry could not penetrate the rugged terrain, remaining road-bound, the Mujahedeen found it comparatively easy to avoid the clumsy efforts of their enemy. As a result Soviet control of the countryside quickly dwindled and the Soviet Fortieth Army lost the initiative. Reduced to garrisoning major cities and protecting logistic networks, the Soviet military force could only react to Mujahedeen threats.

By 1983 the Soviets and their Afghan allies had altered their military tactics, slowly adapting to the irregular nature of the ongoing conflict. Eschewing their reliance on traditional, large-unit operations, the Soviets began to break their forces down into smaller, tactically more versatile formations. Though these smaller units often launched mechanized conventional attacks, they also began to make more liberal use of air power, especially in the form of the helicopter. Air attacks, based on the strength of MiG-21s and Mil-24 Hind helicopter gunships took a heavy toll on guerrilla strength and mobility. Such Soviet strikes were often followed by infantry assaults from Mi-6 Hook helicopters in tactics that closely resembled US air mobility in Vietnam. The strength of the Soviet small-unit operations served to push the Mujahedeen further into the hills, thus 'pacifying' much of the countryside. The liberal use of Soviet firepower and of force, though, was in many ways counterproductive, as it forced ever greater numbers of Afghans to flee the country and provided the Mujahedeen with a never-ending flow of recruits.

Even though the Soviets had achieved some success, the war in Afghanistan dragged on with no end in sight, and the Mujahedeen, though fractured along ethnic and tribal lines, continued to resist. Unlike the Viet Cong during the war in Southeast Asia, the Mujahedeen had no coherent command structure and often engaged in sporadic, uncoordinated operations that had only attrition as their goal. Thus the war settled down into a

ABOVE: American Airborne Rangers guard local revolutionary fighters taken prisoner in Grenada. Though resistance on the island was slight, US forces encountered several worrisome command and control problems.

period of chaotic Mujahedeen guerrilla raids on Soviet interests, including frequent rocket attacks on the capital city of Kabul. Hoping to press their new-found advantage, the Soviets and their Afghan allies began to prosecute air and airmobile attacks on the Mujahedeen supply lines, especially those emanating from Pakistan. The war had entered a new and a dangerous phase.

The Mujahedeen had long received support from and safe haven in Iran and Pakistan: both nations that could stand behind the Afghans in their jihad against the Soviets. However, the continuing war in Afghanistan also drew the attention of the United States. To the Americans, the Afghan War was a part of the wider global struggle of the Cold War and represented a chance for revenge against Soviet support for the North Vietnamese a decade earlier. Thus the United States, led by the CIA, decided to support the Mujahedeen. However, the support was meant as a detriment to Soviet world power, not as support for an Islamic jihad against the West or even for Afghan independence. Thus two of the motive geopolitical forces of the late twentieth century met in Afghanistan: the Cold War and Islamic fundamentalism. The mixture proved quite volatile. American support for the Mujahedeen had remained minimal, just enough to keep the revolution alive as not to destroy the slow warming of relations between East and West. However, the Soviet success in Afghanistan helped to lead to a major US change of policy. Partly in an effort to even the odds in the Afghan War, the US in 1987 began to provide the guerrillas with the very latest in air-defence technology, namely the shoulder-fired, 'Stinger' antiaircraft missiles.

The advent of the Stinger in Afghanistan effectively put an end to Soviet air supremacy and airmobile operations. Most of the Soviet air forces, especially their helicopters, proved to be very vulnerable to Stinger attacks. In fact the first 340 Stingers fired in Afghanistan downed an amazing 269 Soviet aircraft. The balance of the war began to shift yet again. Unable to rely on their helicopters for mobility, the Soviets reverted to less successful tactics of mechanized sweeps.

BELOW: A Soviet soldier guards a convoy during the war in Afghanistan. In spite of a major deployment of forces, the Soviets never managed to achieve total control of the countryside, and the already frequent Mujahedeen attacks on Russian convoys became even more so.

Once again the Mujahedeen found their mountain hideaways safe from most attacks and began to spread their control across the countryside. Soviet and loyal Afghan forces found themselves once again confined to cities and major road networks, as up to 80 per cent of the countryside fell under Mujahedeen control. Also as the war drug on and Soviet fortunes began to dwindle, the morale of their army in Afghanistan began to plummet. Mirroring the Vietnam War after 1968, the Soviet population, amid economic turmoil, began to question the worth of continuing the war in Afghanistan.

RUSSIA'S VIETNAM

With no end to the war in sight, the Soviet military leadership faced a difficult choice: significantly increase the military effort in Afghanistan in search of victory, or seek a negotiated end to the conflict. The new Soviet Premier, Mikhail Gorbachev, fully realized that massive economic and world-wide military challenges faced his beleaguered nation. Even as he began to implement policies such as perestroika, Gorbachev came to the conclusion that he had to put an end to the continued drain represented by the war in Afghanistan. At Soviet direction a new Afghan leader, Mohammed

Najibullah, began to offer economic concessions and even a power-sharing arrangement to the Mujahedeen. Sensing victory and without a unified political voice, the Mujahedeen, though, chose to continue their resistance, and pressed for total victory. Unable to arrange an acceptable peace in Afghanistan, the Soviets chose nevertheless to end their conflict there, removing their last troops from the country on 15 February 1989. Soviet support for the Najibullah regime in Afghanistan continued, as did the war in that country. In 1992, as Soviet support died away, Najibullah surrendered power and the Mujahedeen achieved victory.

During the conflict in Afghanistan Soviet forces had suffered some 14,000 killed and 53,000 wounded, while inflicting millions of casualties upon their tactically overmatched foe. In the end the war had proven unwinnable for the Soviets, pitted against an irregular foe with massive international support. Though they had adapted their tactics the Soviets, in the end, chose withdrawal over escalation of the conflict. The war had been in effect the Soviet's Vietnam. The legacies of the Soviet defeat, however, were even more far-reaching than anyone could have ever expected. Facing unrest in Europe and disaffection at home, the Soviet Union quickly crumbled, bringing

ABOVE: Mujahedeen fighters resting in a safe house in Mazar-e-Sharif. Had the Afghans gone toe-to-toe with the Russians, they would have been slaughtered, no matter how high their religious or nationalist fervour. However, Afghans have been fighting invaders for centuries, and they used guerrilla tactics to frustrate the Soviet colossus.

the Cold War to an end. The military and political realities of the era of limited war and revolution suddenly ceased to exist. The contest of wills between the United States and the Soviet Union had been the motive force behind most wars since World War II and had imposed a series of set rules upon the nature of warfare itself. Suddenly those rules were gone, leaving

ABOVE: Soviet forces firing AGS-17 automatic grenade launching during the conflict in Afghanistan. Such weapons provided them with a light and relatively easy to handle source of direct fire support, a kind of short-range artillery capability.

militaries across the world groping towards a redefinition of modern conflict.

The war in Afghanistan also had several, more hidden results. The success of the Mujahedeen once again seemed to indicate that many future conflicts might assume a more asymmetrical form, often involving bitter struggles between ethnic or religious groupings. Presaging the future, following the fall of the Najibullah government in Afghanistan, peace was not restored to the war-torn nation. Instead the Mujahedeen – never a truly unified force – began to squabble among themselves. Tribal warlords vied for control of the stricken nation, resulting in a thoroughgoing humanitarian tragedy. The United States, having achieved victory in the Cold War, paid little heed to the situation in Afghanistan, seeing it as a regional problem. After years of anarchy, a new unifying force came to the area: fundamentalist Islam in the form of the Taliban. Born of the last conflict of the Cold War era, the growing gap between forces of Islamic fundamentalism and the West came to dominate the emerging conflicts of the 21st century.

THE SEARCH FOR TOMORROW

The loss of the Vietnam War had caused the American military to question its doctrine and indeed the entire American way of war. Since the American Civil War the United States had developed a policy of military attrition in major conflicts, often relying on massive industrial strength to achieve victory. However, such attritional policies had failed in Vietnam and also seemed quite ill-suited to the realities of the ongoing Cold War. Against the Soviet military juggernaut an attritional defence of western Europe seemed doomed to failure and overly reliant on nuclear weapons to redress the strategic balance. Indeed, the major US document concerning the defence of western Europe, Field Manual 100-5 Operations 1976, convinced many US and NATO military theorists that the coming conflict would be a catastrophic defeat. Dissatisfied with the legacy of Vietnam and concerned for the future, American military theorists began to move toward a more aggressive approach towards war, one that relied on manoeuvre and overwhelming firepower aimed at a achieving quick victory.

Even as US military thinkers began to reassess the American way of war, groundbreaking technological changes were sweeping the planet, beginning the computer age and causing what many theorists term a Revolution in Military Affairs. The advent of the microchip in the 1980s revolutionized warfare through an exponential leap forwards in the information available to military commanders, affecting both knowledge of the battlefield and the accuracy of existing and new weapons systems. The new technology, in the main a product of US research and development, allowed commanders an unprecedented 'See Deep' capability. Advanced radar systems aboard E-3 AWACS (Airborne Warning and Control Systems) aircraft could detect all enemy air activity, while E-8 JSTARS (Joint Surveillance and Target Attack Radar Systems) aircraft provided information regarding enemy ground movements. With such information – allowing commanders detailed views of enemy movements up to 1000km (622 miles) behind the front lines – US commanders were able to track enemy troops and air assets long before they reached the front lines. In effect they were capable of seeing up to 96 hours into the future.

'STRIKE DEEP'

Technological advances in weapons systems also provided a new 'Strike Deep' capability. Advanced aircraft such as the F-4G Wild Weasel could disable enemy radar systems, while new Stealth aircraft, such as the F-117A, could avoid enemy radar to launch surprise attacks against enemy forces to their strategic depth. Also a variety of 'stand off' weapons, such as the Cruise Missile, now enabled US forces to attack to strategic depth with little risk to themselves. Much of this new weaponry also used 'smart' technology, including television and laser-guidance systems, to strike targets with previously unseen accuracy. To the layman the strength and variety of the new weapons systems is nearly unimaginable. As an example, a new breed of missile could strike an unsuspecting enemy armoured unit far behind the lines with Wide-Area Anti Armor Munitions (WAAM). The missile disperses several terminally guided submunitions above a battlefield, which then use infrared sensors to locate and strike enemy tanks using a depleted uranium charge. Finally technological developments also provided US commanders with a much more powerful

'Strike Shallow' capability. Along with more traditional forms of firepower, such as tactical bombing, US forces could now even rely on 'smart' artillery shells in the battle for the front lines. The advance in firepower, though, is best illustrated by the advent of the Multiple Launch Rocket System (MLRS). One salvo of 12 rockets from a single MLRS could deliver 8000 M-77 submunitions to the battlefield, devastating a 25,083sq km (30,000 square yard) area.

In the late 1970s, from the command centres of NATO in Europe to training centres in the United States, western military theorists struggled to understand how technology had changed war, and struggled to devise new tactical and strategic doctrines. The culmination of these efforts took place under General Donn Starry at the US Army Training and Doctrine Command, resulting in the issuance of Field Manual 100-5 Operations 1982, a new statement of US military doctrine which was revised in 1986. The doctrine, soon known as AirLand Battle, was meant to apply to any possible war, total or limited, anywhere in the world and aimed at achieving a quick, offensive victory through the use of modern technology and manoeuvre. AirLand Battle took a decisively non-linear view of warfare, envisioning enemy forces and their command structure as a

BELOW: A diagram showing a typical Mujahedeen guerrilla attack on a Soviet convoy. Often attacking in narrow mountain passes, the guerrillas usually tried to disable the lead and trailing vehicles in the column, stranding the remainder. Their task was made easier by the fact that Soviet infantry conscripts almost invariably stayed with their vehicles when attacked, rather than trying to engage the attacking guerrillas in an immediate counterattack.

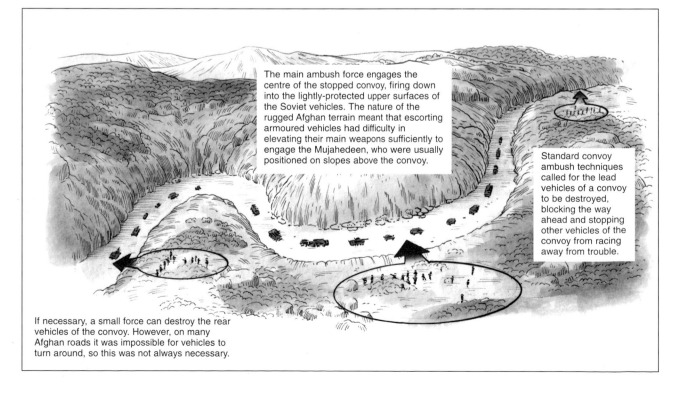

The main ambush force engages the centre of the stopped convoy, firing down into the lightly-protected upper surfaces of the Soviet vehicles. The nature of the rugged Afghan terrain meant that escorting armoured vehicles had difficulty in elevating their main weapons sufficiently to engage the Mujahedeen, who were usually positioned on slopes above the convoy.

Standard convoy ambush techniques called for the lead vehicles of a convoy to be destroyed, blocking the way ahead and stopping other vehicles of the convoy from racing away from trouble.

If necessary, a small force can destroy the rear vehicles of the convoy. However, on many Afghan roads it was impossible for vehicles to turn around, so this was not always necessary.

ABOVE: Soldiers in training for desert warfare during 1991 in Saudi Arabia. Many military pundits thought such training to be of little value, believing that air power alone could win the conflict. No infantryman would have agreed, since history has shown that an enemy was not beaten until he was beaten on the ground.

cyber warfare. Though the use of their unrivalled technology, US forces proposed to out-think, outgun and outmanoeuvre their rivals. AirLand Battle, then, would be the opposite of World War I, for technology this time provided the attacker with all of the advantages. American planners hoped that such an offensive would return decisiveness to warfare, negating the need for protracted wars of attrition. Continued strikes against enemy command and control and logistics would hopefully 'so disrupt the enemy armed forces as to bring about their collapse, psychological and physical, and disintegration'. In essence the US now proposed to fight wars from the inside out. Instead of battering through an opposing army in years of attrition AirLand Battle aimed at the destruction of the 'brain' of the armed forces and the nation, effectively making the enemy's military might on the front lines now totally redundant.

system. Integrating the abilities of the armed forces to an unprecedented extent – especially a blending of air and ground campaigns – AirLand Battle sought to strike an enemy force to strategic depth in variety of ways. The modern battlefield no longer just encompassed the front lines and possibly a strategic bombing campaign. In AirLand Battle US forces proposed to integrate air, ground, sea, space and cyberspace strikes on a new 'integrated battlefield, stretching from ground level to the edge of the atmosphere, from the front line up to 1000 kilometres into the enemy rear, and from the present moment up to 96 hours into the future.'

In a true cataclysm of modern war, the defender would face attack at all levels, from MLRS salvos on the front lines to destruction of command and control to

Many US and NATO military theorists saw AirLand Battle as revolutionary, making all other forms of war and the humble infantryman obsolete. However, there remained high levels of trepidation concerning the new style of war. Reliant on vulnerable and costly technology, AirLand Battle called for an unprecedented and seemingly impossible level of all-arms coordination and information management. Wars involving AirLand Battle would be costly and would require hitherto unseen levels of

RIGHT: Soldiers of the US 101st Air Assault Division in action during 'Operation Desert Storm'. Although tanks and aircraft were the stars of the war against Saddam Hussein, it was the humble infantry who had to take and hold ground until the Iraqis surrendered.

training for and professionalism from soldiers. In addition AirLand Battle was an offensive doctrine, and as such involved great risks for great gains. Thus while some military commanders were lauding AirLand Battle as the wave of the future, others considered it over-ambitious, and they voiced doubts about whether it would work at all.

THE GULF WAR

The initial test of AirLand Battle came in a quite unexpected way. Iraq, under the dictatorial leadership of Saddam Hussein, had long sought more influence in the affairs of the Middle East. In an inconclusive, but bloody struggle with Iran (1980–1988) Iraq had suffered great economic losses and soon sought to recoup those losses at the expense of a lesser foe. Though the Iraqi military was the fourth largest military in the world and was battle tested, it was also fatally flawed. The vast majority of the Iraqi Army consisted of unenthusiastic and poorly trained conscripts who were often quite divided in their ethnic and religious loyalties. As in most dictatorships, Saddam considered his own mass army something of a threat and gave the best of training and equipment only to his most loyal units, including the Republican Guard and the Haras al Ra'is al-Khas. In many ways these units, though by far Saddam's most capable, were too valuable to use in battle, for they also served as his insurance policy against his own people. Though strong on paper – and having learned much from the war with Iran – Iraq's Army was poorly suited for a struggle with a modern western armed force.

The deficiencies of the Iraqi Army mattered little, for their opponent was tiny Kuwait. Totally misreading the situation, Saddam was quite certain that the western Allies would not involve themselves in the coming war. After OPEC failed to placate Iraq by increasing the price of oil, in August 1990 the Iraqi armed forces moved forwards into Kuwait in a daring and unexpected offensive. The tiny sultanate had few defences and quickly fell to the invader, giving Iraq control over 15 per cent of the world's oil reserves. Though Arab nations sought to solve the problem themselves, the nations of the west – dependant on Middle East oil – remained

quite frightened that Iraqi forces might push into Saudi Arabia in a bid for control of over 40 per cent of the world's oil. Saddam had, thus, misjudged the level of world interest in his actions and had also chosen the wrong time for such actions. With the end of the Cold War the US and NATO could take military action in the Middle East without fear of Soviet intervention or an unwanted escalation of the conflict. The abatement of Cold War rivalries also made it possible for the United Nations Security Council to adopt a stance calling upon all member nations to oppose the invasion of Kuwait. Finally Saddam had believed that Arab disunity and hatred of Israel would help to serve as a buffer to outside military interference in the region. Once again he was mistaken and soon was quite surprised to witness the formation of a world-wide coalition, which was aimed at the liberation of Kuwait.

Having made the decision to fight, the nations of the coalition now had to gather defensive forces in Saudi Arabia in 'Operation Desert Shield'. In this quite dangerous phase of the war the coalition – including some 30 countries providing naval units, seven providing air units and eight providing ground units – had to mass their forces from all over the globe and transport them to the Middle East. Though the operation in the end went smoothly, it was in many ways a logistical nightmare, one that would have nearly been insurmountable had Saddam chosen to attack. The Iraqi leader, however, chose not to push into Saudi Arabia, instead opting to build massive defensive networks throughout Kuwait, hoping that coalition forces would balk at fighting a war that resembled the defensive struggle of the Iran-Iraq War. Several outside observers agreed that the coming war would be long and bloody. Though estimates varied, it seemed that Iraq had gathered a considerable force in Kuwait numbering some 500,000 men, 4300 tanks (including 500 modern Soviet T-72s), 3000 artillery pieces, 400 aircraft and hundreds of Soviet SS-1 Scud B missiles, possibly tipped with biological or chemical warheads. The force was indeed powerful, but nonetheless poorly motivated, and occupied forward defences which were almost uniquely susceptible to attack by AirLand Battle.

ABOVE: Two US Marine riflemen serving with a reconnaissance platoon keep watch on enemy movements during 'Operation Desert Storm'. The Marine at left is a sniper, armed with an M-40A1 rifle. His companion acts as the spotter, identifying targets for the shooter.

Though several nations took part in the campaign, making command and control uniquely difficult, the United States provided the majority of the forces for the conflict. President George Bush, once the decision for war had been made, left most of the military planning to his trusted military subordinates: General Colin Powell, Chairman of the Joint Chiefs of Staff, and General H. Norman Schwarzkopf, Commander-in-Chief of US Central Command. Both were veterans of the Vietnam War.

While the massive coalition force slowly gathered together in Saudi Arabia Schwarzkopf directed that the Pentagon plan an air campaign against Iraq. The resulting scheme, initially dubbed 'Instant Thunder', called for a massive air campaign prosecuted to enemy strategic depth that would last only nine days, but would cause the immediate defeat of Iraq and the withdrawal of their forces from Kuwait. Thus the faith exhibited by Pentagon planners in the air component of AirLand Battle was so profound that they believed a ground war to be unnecessary. Schwarzkopf and Powell, though, thought differently and overruled their planners. The resultant coalition plan of action called for a six-week sustained air campaign against Iraq, under the control of General Charles Horner. The aerial offensive would use the

massive array of coalition technology to strike at Iraqi command and control, telecommunications and logistic infrastructure and was aimed at decapitating the Iraqi forces in Kuwait. A later goal of the air campaign would be the massed carpet-bombing of Iraqi forces in Kuwait in preparation for the final and huge ground offensive.

Having gathered together some 2600 military aircraft in the Persian Gulf area, on the night of 17 January 1991 the coalition began its air campaign, the first phase of 'Operation Desert Storm'. With air supremacy as a first goal, coalition forces had utilized electronic surveillance to locate the Iraqi 'Kari' air-defence system along with the Air Defence Operations Centre in Baghdad and subsidiary air-defence centres throughout the region. US Special Forces guided AH-64 Apache helicopters to the forward air-defence sights, which destroyed the targets using Hellfire guided missiles. At the same time, Stealth fighters and 54 cruise missiles struck the Air Defence Operations Centre in Baghdad. In addition, EF-111 Raven aircraft eliminated most resistance from Iraqi Surface-to-Air Missile sites.

After a night of fighting, Iraq's air defences had been totally compromised, at the cost of one coalition aircraft lost. Saddam resorted to desperate measures in

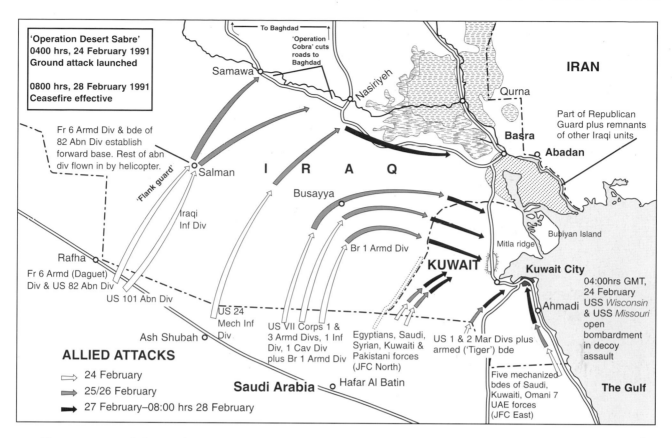

'Operation Desert Sabre'
0400 hrs, 24 February 1991
Ground attack launched

0800 hrs, 28 February 1991
Ceasefire effective

To Baghdad

'Operation Cobra' cuts roads to Baghdad

IRAN

Samawa

Nasiriyeh

Qurna

Basra

Abadan

Part of Republican Guard plus remnants of other Iraqi units

Fr 6 Armd Div & bde of 82 Abn Div establish forward base. Rest of abn div flown in by helicopter.

Salman

I R A Q

'Flank guard'

Iraqi Inf Div

Busayya

Bubiyan Island

Mitla ridge

Kuwait City

Rafha

Fr 6 Armd (Daguet) Div & US 82 Abn Div

US 101 Abn Div

Br 1 Armd Div

KUWAIT

Ahmadi

04:00hrs GMT, 24 February USS *Wisconsin* & USS *Missouri* open bombardment in decoy assault

US 24 Mech Inf Div

US VII Corps 1 & 3 Armd Divs, 1 Inf Div, 1 Cav Div plus Br 1 Armd Div

Egyptians, Saudi, Syrian, Kuwaiti & Pakistani forces (JFC North)

US 1 & 2 Mar Divs plus armed ('Tiger') bde

Ash Shubah

ALLIED ATTACKS

⟹ 24 February

⟹ 25/26 February

⟹ 27 February–08:00 hrs 28 February

Saudi Arabia

Hafar Al Batin

Five mechanized bdes of Saudi, Kuwaiti, Omani 7 UAE forces (JFC East)

The Gulf

an effort to restore balance, firing Scud missiles blindly at Saudi Arabia and Israel in an effort to rend the coalition asunder. The Scuds, though rather ineffective, caused great worry to coalition planners, for aircraft and Special Forces both had great difficulty in locating and destroying mobile Scud launchers, demonstrating a weakness in the tapestry of technological warfare. Even so, the air war over Iraq was over, as evidenced when many Iraqi fighters flew to Iran for internment.

Next the air campaign moved on to the destruction of Iraqi command, logistics and ability to wage war. The violent, and now virtually unopposed attacks achieved great success, shutting down 88 per cent of the Iraqi national electrical grid, destroying 90 per cent of the Iraqi ability to refine oil, and lowering the flow of supplies coming into Kuwait from 75,000 tons per day to 16,000 tons per day. Air attack also played a vital role in preparing the battlefield, destroying a claimed 32 per cent of Iraq's armoured vehicles and 47 per cent of its artillery before the launch of the ground campaign. Though these numbers remain in doubt, the air assault played a vital role in the coming coalition success in the Gulf War. Air war theorists continued to hope that the bombing campaign would break the back

of Iraq, negating the need for a ground war, but the Iraqis held on stubbornly in the face of heavy losses. Indeed the air war had actually achieved less than AirLand Battle plans had stipulated, for the enemy had not been decapitated or collapsed. Part of this shortfall is due to the fact that western militaries were not yet ready to prosecute a true AirLand campaign. Only some seven per cent of the munitions fired in the Gulf War were precision-guided. Even so, the air campaign cost $1.3 billion, a testament to the cost of modern weapons systems.

ABOVE: After a feint towards Kuwait City, US and British forces attacked in a 'left hook' aimed at cutting off all Iraqi retreat.

BELOW: A US soldier speeds down a desert track during the Gulf War. Coalition superiority in mechanization and technology provided a decisive edge over the numerous but overmatched Iraqi armed forces.

ABOVE: The US Army's Objective Individual Combat Weapon (OICW) combines an advanced sighting system incorporating a thermal imager and a laser rangefinder with an experimental 20mm (0.78in.) grenade launcher and a 5.56mm (0.22in.) assault rifle. It will allow 21st Century soldiers to attack hidden targets more accurately from safer distances.

road from Kuwait to Baghdad. With supplies often being flown in before their arrival, the remainder of XVIII Corps advanced quickly, finally managing to seal the coalition flank from any oncoming danger from the enemy.

It remained for VII Corps to seal the victory in the Gulf by defeating the Iraqi Republican Guard, which was held in a theatre reserve. VII Corps numbered over 145,000 men, as well as a total of 40,000 vehicles which consumed some 5.6 million gallons of fuel every day. Fighting for VII Corps remained rather sparse, as most Republican Guard units chose to retreat and avoid battle. However, on 25 February, VII Corps encountered several elements of two Iraqi armoured units. The two sides fought a sharp battle amid a blinding, howling sandstorm.

During the fighting, it became quite obvious that the US M1A1 Abrams outclassed all of the Iraqi tanks. Using thermal rangefinders and a substantial advantage in range, the American tanks made short work of their adversaries, destroying hundreds of Iraqi tanks and, in the process, managing to avoid suffering a single loss. On 27 February, with Iraqi resistance on a steady decline, forward elements of VII Corps reached their goal: the Basra-Kuwait City Highway, cutting off the most obvious means of Iraqi retreat, leading to an official cessation of hostilities on the following day.

The Gulf War has its critics, and in many ways it did not represent a true test of AirLand Battle. Many Iraqi units were able to escape the technological trap and escape to the north, where they succeed to this day in maintaining Saddam Hussein as the Iraqi leader. The Gulf War was not, however, intended as a total war, and AirLand Battle had won its quick, resounding victory. It was then time for the politicians to take charge of the peace negotiations.

The casualty rates during the Gulf War were astounding, serving to overcome any criticism and also seeming to herald a true revolution in warfare. During the conflict, the Iraqis had lost a total of some 200,000 dead, 200,000 deserted and 50,000 prisoners. Total coalition casualties stood at less than 1000 killed and wounded. The Iraqis also lost some 3700 tanks and 2000 artillery pieces as a result of the war against the Allies.

By 24 February 1991 there were nearly 545,000 coalition forces in the Kuwaiti Theatre of Operations (KTO). After months of planning, Schwarzkopf decided to employ a two-stage strategy. Initially coalition forces would feign a frontal advance into Kuwait and an amphibious landing at Kuwait City. After locking Iraqi attention on the area, over 250,000 coalition forces – mainly the US VII and XVIII Corps – shifted in a westerly direction in order to prosecute a 'left hook', an armoured flank sweep through the Iraqi desert which would be covered by airmobile units.

On the morning of 24 February, coalition forces rolled forward, and even those forces facing the strength of the Iraqi defences made considerable headway at little cost, often finding their greatest difficulty was caring for the masses of prisoners who surrendered to anything that moved, including drone aircraft and journalists. On the extreme left XVIII Corps raced through the Iraqi desert, preceded by an airmobile operation by the 101st Airborne some 275km (171 miles) into Iraq that cut the

To most observers these numbers were conclusive. It seemed that technology had returned decisiveness to war. Air power, smart munitions, stand off weaponry, and quality armour were able to render even the most powerful defences ineffective. The revolutionary nature of the Gulf War victory seemed to indicate that total war was now a thing of the past, and indeed warfare in general might be outdated, for no nation was able to stand against the technological might of the West. Once again, observers proclaimed that the end of infantry warfare was at hand.

FUTURE INFANTRY

Some military theorists, despairing of the further usefulness of infantry in war, advocated bringing the infantryman up to date through further technological developments. One theorist stated that, 'In the end the rifle-bearing infantryman is governed by the same principles that governed the spear hurler and the bowman – first see the target, then try to get your hands to direct your projectile toward it.' This was certainly a quaint anachronism on the modern-day battlefield.

Several US planners began a series of tests and programs to update infantry, including the development of 'The Enhanced Integrated Soldier's System'. The ultra-modern infantryman was to wear body armour as well as a heads-up display, virtual reality helmet, which would allow for full night vision and instantaneous cyber communications. Carrying laser designators and global positioning equipment, the soldier could call in an attack by smart weapons on any designated target.

In the most advanced suggested systems, a soldier would only have to look at a target, before his onboard computer systems, using laser optics, would focus in on the target and then fire a variety of hand-held smart weapons. Such a variety of weaponry might be quite heavy so there was a scheme, code-named PITMAN, to develop an infantry robotic exoskeleton to make the wearer more powerful.

The advocates of technology, though, expected far too much from the Revolution in Military Affairs. Certainly the Gulf War represented a resounding victory for technology in war, but even

it was incomplete. Technological changes have continued, though not at the pace that many had thought, making the armies of the west even more lethal, and expensive. As prices of weapons systems continue to skyrocket, many now wonder whether technological war is not the wave of the future, for only one country can afford to prosecute such war. And even the mighty United States could not prosecute a truly technological war for an extended period of time.

Additionally the success of the Gulf War seems to have convinced 'rogue nations' throughout the world that they should not face the West in such a conflict ever again. Taking the lesson that for every technological advance there is a 'dumb' solution, rogue nations have altered the rules of warfare once again. Rather than becoming more technological, since the Gulf War wars have become less so, involving bloody ethnic conflicts, religious wars and terror strikes. If the combatants hide among the people – or even are the people – technology is foiled, and war becomes, once again, the purview of the infantryman.

BELOW: Though a 'Revolution in Military Affairs' seemed to beckon after the Gulf War, it is still the humble infantryman that takes and holds ground. Indeed, as engineers rush to develop countermeasures against high-tech armoured and aerial wonder weapons, the place of the infantryman will become more, not less, important in future wars.

CHAPTER TEN

PEACE-KEEPING

As the end of the Cold War reduced the threat of global conflict, it released a myriad of new challenges to the world's armies. These ranged from peacemaking and peacekeeping to dealing with the terrorist threat.

The United Nations (UN) was founded in an era of great international insecurity following fast on the heels of World War II. The war had been caused, in many ways, by Hitler's rise to prominence during a period of appeasement, something that many political theorists believed could have been prevented by strong international action. Post-war political and military planners worldwide believed that international collective security, represented in the UN, could limit future conflicts and reign in rogue states, averting the threat of World War III. As the Cold War persisted and the world began to line up in two armed camps, the role of the UN as peacemaker became magnified. Though it had no standing armed force, the UN, under the executive direction of the Security Council, possessed the vast if somewhat nebulous power to intervene in international affairs. However, the inner workings of the Security Council itself served to place a buffer on UN assertion of authority. As permanent members of the Security Council, both the United States and the Soviet Union possessed absolute veto power, something that both nations used with great abandon during the Cold War era. In essence the continued superpower rivalry served to

LEFT: On peacekeeping missions, soldiers are often used to maintain law and order. These paratroopers from the US Army's 504th Parachute Infantry Regiment are helping United Nations' police as they move down an alley in Mitrovica, Kosovo, in February 2000. They are conducting a house-to-house search for weapons.

make the UN ineffective in its major goal. Thus as the Cold War itself and the threat of nuclear destruction placed limits on wars, the UN searched long and hard for its own identity.

Even as the US and the Soviet Union contested for world domination in the Cold War, other forces such as decolonization threatened world peace outside the spheres of direct superpower influence. Though there were no provisions for such actions in its charter, the UN began to take part in peacekeeping missions throughout the world in an effort to monitor several troublespots. The beginnings of what is now known as 'traditional peacekeeping' took place in 1948 when UN forces went to Palestine as impartial observers to monitor the truce between the Palestinians and Israelis. Limited by Cold War rivalry until 1990, the UN would muster some 13 peacekeeping missions across the globe, from the Congo to Lebanon to New Guinea. The nature of the missions varied widely but followed a set pattern. The UN, under the leadership of Dag Hammarskjold, would only send forces into an area with the consent of the belligerent parties involved. Thus the UN would not make peace or force peace on nations, but would only monitor and promote peace agreements that had already been reached. UN peacekeeping forces were small and lightly armed and only used force in self-defence. Hammarskjold also strove to maintain UN impartiality and would not draw peacekeeping forces from any of the five permanent members of the Security Council. Following these guidelines, though UN forces served under difficult circumstances in many of the most dangerous parts of the world, their peacekeeping operations were to achieve several marked successes.

The close of the Cold War brought fundamental change to the peacekeeping process. The lessening of East–West rivalries opened much more of the world to direct United Nations influence, allowing peacekeepers roles in nations that had been Cold War hotspots, including Namibia and Cambodia. Also the Security Council became a 'vcto free environment', removing all artificial controls on the expansion of peacekeeping missions. Combined with

BELOW: Peacekeepers often found themselves isolated in the midst of brutal civil struggles. These members of the 709th Military Police Battalion have been surrounded by a hostile crowd in Sevce, Kosovo on 4 April 2000. Several hundred Serbs blocked the road to protest at the arrest earlier in the day of a local suspected of possessing munitions.

the development of a geopolitical atmosphere conducive to peacekeeping, the end of the Cold War created increased the need for peacekeeping missions. Superpower rivalry, often in support of brutal, but ideologically compatible regimes, had done much to control lesser ethnic, tribal and religious rivalries in countries across the globe. With the end of the Cold War, though, the superpowers lost interest in nations of once great strategic importance, including Somalia and Afghanistan. Without artificial controls, several nations overthrew their Cold War leadership only to dissolve into the anarchy of tribal and ethnic warfare. At an alarming rate, nations from Europe to Africa began to implode, leading to brutal civil conflict and humanitarian disasters. As a result, UN peacekeeping activity throughout the world increased greatly, and in 1994 there were 17 UN operations ongoing involving 85,000 personnel from 70 different nations.

UN PEACEKEEPERS

Most importantly, though, the role of UN peacekeepers in the post-Cold War world began to change. The new UN Secretary General, Boutros Boutros-Ghali, sought to seize the moment, seeing the UN as the 'beacon for a new planetary order'. In

the new world environment there were few interstate conflicts for the UN to mediate. Instead peacekeeping missions would enter the realm of unstable internal ethnic and civil wars. In such confused, dangerous situations there were often no true local authorities that could offer their consent to peacekeeping missions, thus raising the possibility of attacks on UN forces. Also, continued anarchy in several countries led Boutros-Ghali to believe that UN forces should sometimes intervene in the affairs of sovereign nations without invitation to prevent humanitarian disasters. Such operations, sometimes known as peacemaking missions, were, 'carried out to restore peace between belligerent parties who do not all consent to intervention and may be engaged in combat activities.' Peacemaking forces had to be large and well armed, ready to do combat in the midst of a bewildering swirl of societal violence and decay. The size and nature of such missions also changed the nature of peacekeeping by requiring the involvement of the last remaining superpower. The involvement of American forces in peacekeeping missions represented a major departure from traditional peacekeeping. To many nations in the Third World the presence

ABOVE. Not all contacts with locals are hostile. Staff Sergeant John J. McCarthy of the US Army's 315th Psychological Operations Company, and his interpreter talk to a Kosovar Serb man after giving him a copy of *Dialog* – a KFOR publication printed in Serbo-Croatian and Albanian, on 4 May 2000 – in the Novo Brdo Obstina, Kosovo.

ABOVE: A Czech peacekeeper mans a checkpoint in Bosnia in 1996. The seemingly endless sequence of conflicts in the Balkans marked the first occasion in which former Warsaw Pact forces were under the same command as NATO units.

the Cold War, though, superpower interest in the region lapsed, forcing the government of Somalia to stand on its own. Without controls imposed by the superpower rivalry, disparate Somali factions banded together in opposition to the Barre government, forcing its eventual collapse in the beginning of 1991. In the resulting societal chaos several warlords and ethnic groupings vied for control of the stricken nation. Buying arms on the vast world market Somali warlords – representative of several coming struggles in the post-Cold War era – relied in the main on militia forces for their power. These infantrymen, often including children, received little training or discipline. As a result the warring factions often seemed to be little more than thugs, caring little for life or the rules of war. From Rwanda to Kosovo such armed groups would engage in a seemingly never-ending escalation of slaughter and revenge, usually termed ethnic cleansing. The leaders of such groups, including Mohammed Farah Aydeed, often thought only of their own welfare, and retained only nominal control over their deadly bands. Such situations were fraught with danger for peacemakers, for the lack of law and order or real rulers meant there could never be true consent.

By late 1992 it had become obvious to the outside world that famine had struck Somalia in the wake of the anarchy there, leading to a humanitarian disaster. As the situation worsened and over a million people neared starvation, though the war in Somalia continued, the UN decided to intervene. In September 1992 a small force of UN peacekeepers arrived in Somalia to help secure delivery of international aid shipments to the starving local population. However, Somali warlords, especially Aydeed, viewed the UN intervention with suspicion and as something of an opportunity. Armed bands would regularly steal food shipments for their own uses and the humanitarian disaster worsened. Plainly the UN needed more military punch in Somalia. For the upgraded peacemaking effort, several nations committed troops, but the United States took the lead by offering a force of 30,000 men in an attempt to overawe the recalcitrant Somali warlords.

of American forces did much to diminish the supposed impartiality of the UN, leading to the possibility of interstate conflict with the US. In addition American forces, now trained to 'fight to win' would often see peacemaking in different way to the way the UN leadership would see it.

SOMALIA

The collapse of the East African nation of Somalia offered a stern test for the proponents of peacemaking. During the 1980s the United States had supported the dictatorial Somali regime of Siyad Barre, in part to offset Soviet influence in neighbouring Ethiopia. After the end of

Reflecting the new realities of peacemaking, the UN initially, in most ways, lost control of its mission in Somalia to the world's remaining superpower. Beginning 'Operation Restore Hope' US Marines landed on the beach outside Mogadishu on the morning of 9 March 1993 and were greeted by a phalanx of representatives of the news media. Within days the peacekeepers had taken control of parts of Mogadishu as well as much of the surrounding countryside.

Initially the mission went well and resulted in the effective distribution of aid to the grateful Somalis. However, to many in the UN and the US, such a situation seemed to be only a temporary palliative. Once the peacekeepers left, the anarchy would surely return, bringing with it the humanitarian disaster. At this point the nature of the UN/US mission began to change from one of dispensing humanitarian aid to a mission of disarming Somali militias and bringing an end to the war. The Somali warlords chose to resist, thus leading the peacemaking mission gradually to change into an undeclared urban guerrilla war.

Humanitarian aid and peacemaking are highly involved personal missions and as such are the purview of the infantryman. Even in a situation with the consent of the parties involved, the task of the peacekeeper is quite difficult, requiring tact and forbearance more often than military might. Even in such situations violence often erupts, leaving the lightly armed and usually outnumbered peacekeepers to rely on their personal training and initiative for their very survival. In situations such as that seen in Somalia, though, the task of the infantryman was infinitely more problematic than this. Still needing to maintain the humanitarian mission, small infantry units – often in trucks or all-terrain vehicles – would often find themselves in a sea of people while navigating the narrow streets of Mogadishu. Dealing with such situations is quite difficult, often requiring very specific training in crowd- and riot control. Adding to this problem, Aydeed's militiamen could be anywhere, just waiting to launch a guerrilla attack. Thus some peacekeepers compared their position to that of a 'living target'.

BELOW: A Canadian Coyote reconnaissance vehicle passes a column of British Challenger main battle tanks in Kosovo. NATO forces are used to joint operations, but the multi-national nature of peacekeeping forces can see forces with very different standards of training serving alongside one another in a foreign location, making for a potential command and control nightmare.

On 5 June the simmering war in Mogadishu exploded when Aydeed's forces ambushed a group of Pakistani peacekeepers, killing 23 in a confused and brutal struggle. Dismayed, UN Secretary General Boutros-Ghali called for the arrest of Aydeed and the implied destruction of his militia group. For the first time UN forces had intervened in the affairs of a sovereign nation and chosen sides in a civil war. Frustrated by the development, some of the UN contingents, notably the Italians, expressed their displeasure at what was happening, but operations continued. Several violent skirmishes took place, but UN forces were unable to locate the elusive Somali warlord.

During August élite US forces, including Delta Force and the 75th Rangers, arrived in Mogadishu to prosecute the capture of Aydeed and his chief lieutenants. The UN forces, though, were at a disadvantage that would become typical to peacekeepers. The small size of the elite units and the potential of danger to the population of Mogadishu precluded the use of main force. Also Aydeed was in his element, surrounded by supporters in an insular culture, thus making intelligence-gathering concerning his movements difficult to control. Thus in many ways the UN and US forces struck blindly into

Mogadishu, eventually serving only to unite the population against the now coercive UN and US presence.

On 3 October an impasse was reached in the war in Somalia. Members of Delta Force and the 75th Rangers attempted to capture several Aydeed lieutenants in a 'snatch raid'. The raid was meant to be lighting quick, utilizing the speed and power of helicopters. Though the operation began well, Aydeed's forces used rocket-propelled grenades to down two US helicopters. Hundreds of Aydeed supporters rushed to the scene to attack the stranded, surrounded Americans.

Exhibiting command and control problems common to multinational missions, UN response forces with tanks languished at their base while a company of the US 10th Mountain Division attempted to rush to the aid of their compatriots in trucks, only to stumble into an ambush. Finally the UN relief column, led by Pakistani tanks, reached the scene, but the battle was in the main already over. During the struggle 18 American peacekeepers died and 100 were wounded. Estimates contend that 300 Somalis died in the struggle.

After the battle President Bill Clinton began to withdraw American troops from Somalia, leaving the Somalis to find their own solutions to their problems. By March 1995 all UN forces had

BELOW: The first contingent of US Marines from the 26th Marine Expeditionary Unit load on to a CH-53D Sea Stallion helicopter on the deck of the USS *Kearsarge* (LHD 3) as the ship operates in the Adriatic Sea on 8 June 1999. The Marines are heading to a staging area in Skopje, Macedonia, in support of NATO's 'Operation Allied Force'.

LEFT: Italian peacekeepers man their M109 155mm (6.1in.) howitzers outside Sarajevo. Though the UN had intended its operations in Bosnia to be merely humanitarian in nature, 'mission creep' slowly set in, putting UN troops on the road towards open conflict in the area.

withdrawn from Somalia and the Somali warlords were left to fight a bitter battle over possession of the abandoned UN compound in Mogadishu.

The failure of 'Operation Restore Hope' illustrated the dangers of post-Cold War peacemaking and would and set the precedent for most UN actions to follow. The UN operation had changed from one of humanitarian aid to an undeclared war against one faction in a civil war. The dangers of peacekeeping or peacemaking in still violent situations had caused the UN to take sides in the struggle, thus losing much of its moral authority. The precedent for the infantryman was sobering indeed. Asked to perform as humanitarian aid-workers rather than fighters, the task of the infantry was both frustrating and imminently dangerous. When the task transformed to war, the infantry found itself operating under a fragmented command structure, with little available force, all while becoming the central villain in a brutal civil war.

BELOW: Unlike in many previous UN peacekeeping operations, which were often carried out by lightly equipped troops, the NATO force in Bosnia was heavily armed with state-of-the-art weaponry. NATO made it clear to the Serbs that vehicles like this powerful Italian Centauro armoured car were not for show: they would be used if necessary.

BOSNIA

The collapse of Yugoslavia presented the UN with a critical test of its humanitarian role in the midst of a civil war that resulted in a societal holocaust. In 1992 citizens of Bosnia, following the example set by Slovenia and Croatia, voted to support independence from Yugoslavia, a nation dominated by the state of Serbia. The population of Bosnia, though, was ethnically divided: 44 per cent Muslim Slavs, 31 per cent Serbs and 17 per cent Croats. Quickly the tiny nation fell into a three-sided civil war as the major ethnic groupings vied for control. However, the largest group, the Muslims, soon found themselves at a distinct disadvantage, for the Serbs and the Croats could both rely on support from neighbouring ethnically supportive nations. As the crisis deepened, the UN made the situation worse by declaring an arms embargo on the region, an embargo that only had any real effect on the Muslims. Soon the Serbs gained the upper hand in the civil war, seizing over 70 per cent of the countryside and laying siege to several Muslim cities, including Sarajevo. By 1993 it had become obvious that the Serbs were engaging in an ethnic cleansing of Bosnia, horrifically displacing and killing millions of Muslims.

Against the backdrop of continued slaughter the UN did little, merely hoping that European intervention would solve the problem. Also, as the situation in Somalia worsened, Boutros-Ghali worried that any UN intervention in Bosnia would only serve to add a fourth participant to the ongoing war. Much more so than Somalia, there was no peace to keep in Bosnia, making humanitarian aid or peacemaking extremely difficult. Even so, Boutros-Ghali chose to send a small force to Bosnia to ensure the distribution of humanitarian aid, especially in beleaguered Sarajevo. In 1993 the UN declared a 'no-fly zone' over Bosnia in an effort to halt Serb air strikes.

However, the UN possessed little ability to enforce such a decision and relied on NATO for support. The alliance between the UN and NATO remained quite uneasy as UN forces concentrated on their humanitarian efforts, while NATO forces – often in direct violation of Security Council instructions – began to

BELOW: During the conflict in Sierra Leone peacekeeping forces once again found themselves vulnerable in the face of a societal holocaust, caught between ill-disciplined warring factions who had lost all semblance of restraint.

strike Serb units on the ground. Thus the UN mission in Bosnia had started to shift towards peacemaking, but with NATO as the spearhead and the driving force.

In 1994 the fighting in Bosnia began to centre around several Muslim strongholds that the UN had declared safe havens. During April the Serb refusal to halt attacks on the safe haven of Gorazde resulted in a NATO air attack on Serb positions, forcing compliance. Shortly thereafter NATO aircraft also bombed the area around Sarajevo. Though the war had escalated, involving the first combat operations ever by NATO forces, the bitter ethnic fighting continued. Serb forces sometimes complied with UN regulations, even going to the extent of turning over some of their heavy weaponry to UN control. However, more often than not, the Serbs fought on, even taking UN troops hostage in order to further their harsh struggle.

By 1995 it had become clear that UN humanitarian missions and sporadic NATO strikes would have little effect on the situation as a whole. Serb pressure on the safe havens increased to the point where in August 1995 UN forces

abandoned Srebrenica, which shortly fell to advancing Serbs. The resultant slaughter of civilians in the area forced a UN and NATO change of strategy.

Determined to bring the war in Bosnia under control, NATO had already begun to bring combat ground forces into the area. Led by the British 24th Airmobile Brigade, NATO troops hoped to be able to act as a rapid response force that could quickly come to the aid of any UN peacekeeping units that had fallen under Serb attack. Some NATO leaders argued that the commitment of troops would cross the 'Mogadishu Line', moving from a peacekeeping role to participation in an escalating civil war.

The dynamic in Bosnia, though, was quite different, for UN forces worked hard to maintain their neutrality, while NATO forces represented a mailed fist and an escalation of the conflict. After the fall of Srebrenica the regional dynamics shifted dramatically. NATO forces, pushing aside UN desires and control, embarked upon a sustained air and artillery offensive against the Serbs, dubbed 'Operation Deliberate Force'. The façade of peacekeeping had been

ABOVE: Unlike the situation in the Balkans, the UN force in Sierra Leone is largely composed of units from armies like India, Bangladesh and Nigeria. Command is divided, though the force is the only thing preventing a further descent into anarchy. Several hundred British troops have provided training and leadership for government forces, but they do not come under United Nations' command.

dropped, and forceful peacemaking was now the international goal. The operation was quite unlike that seen in Somalia, and represented a more standard form of warfare. Using techniques perfected in the Gulf War, NATO aircraft punished the static Serb positions. With few restrictions, NATO was able to put its massive edge in firepower to good use, again unlike the cramped streets of Mogadishu. Reeling from years of civil war and taking a relentless pounding from NATO attacks, the Serbs finally relented, resulting in the December 1995 signing of the Dayton Peace Accord. Bosnia would settle down into an uneasy

ABOVE: Rather than being a technological wonder war, the 'War Against Terror' blends the ultra-modern, with the old. Here, US Special Forces troops ride on horseback as they work with members of the Northern Alliance in Afghanistan during the early stages of 'Operation Enduring Freedom' in 2001.

period of peace. For their part, UN forces would now assume the task of monitoring the agreement, thereby returning to a much more successful pattern of traditional peacekeeping.

As the world enters the 21st century, it seems that the implosion of nations and resulting ethnic violence and humanitarian disasters will continue without abatement. In response, though the UN has attempted to return to a more traditional role of peacekeeping, forceful peacemaking missions will become more common. The new paradigm of peacemaking was demonstrated once again in the recent conflict in Sierra Leone. After a period of anarchy and civil war, the warring factions in Sierra Leone – again ill-controlled, ruthless groups of civilian

solders – reached a tentative peace to be monitored by UN peacekeepers. Once again, though, the clarity of the UN mission began to blur, leading to 'mission creep' towards open conflict with the main rebel faction, the RUF, and resulting in a British intervention in the growing conflict. In such situations, where lack of consent regarding peacekeeping leads to conflict, the UN has come to rely on outside intervention, ranging from US to NATO to British support. This shift in policy implementation indicates that the UN and the nations of the West will have to work ever more closely across the planet. However, such an alliance is often counterproductive, convincing the nations of the Third World that the UN is controlled by, and works for, US and western interests. In the resulting struggles it will be the infantryman – in the role of peacekeeper or peacemaker – who bears the burden of the fighting.

THE WAR AGAINST TERROR

After the victory in the Cold War the United States, the lone world superpower, sought to create a 'new world order', one alternately viewed as peaceful or hegemonic, depending on regional geopolitical realities. In the wake of events in Afghanistan and the Middle East – and partly dependent upon the supposed control of the UN by the West – leaders of ethnic, religious and regional struggles began to identify the US and its western Allies as legitimate military targets. As nations continued to implode and regional strife escalated, it seemed quite logical to turn against the leaders of the new world order and to view the system as a failure and a threat.

The crushing western victory in the Gulf War, though, indicated that it would be foolhardy to stand against the might of the United States in open battle. Thus new, disaffected groups – often without the organized support of a national unit – chose to strike at western interests using asymmetrical warfare and terrorism. Often cloaked in the language of fundamentalist Islam, these new military groupings sought to change the reality of modern warfare yet again by using guerrilla and terror tactics to defeat the western edge in firepower and technology. The coming conflict would once again focus on the initiative and perseverance of individual soldiers: it would be an infantryman's war.

Terrorism is usually defined as the use of violence against civilians by revolutionary organizations in an effort to coerce those civilians or their governments. Though terrorism as such has existed throughout the history of armed conflict, it only became an international phenomenon after the establishment of a communist revolutionary ideology. Believing in the revolutionary 'propaganda of the deed' Marxists from Lenin to Che Guevara believed that violent attacks against the government or its supporters could help facilitate the onset of widespread revolutions. Arguably Carlos Marighela stands as the most important modern terrorist theorist. In his *Minimanual of Urban Guerrilla Warfare*, Marighela contends that 'unbridled violence by a fanatical few, regardless of the apparent likelihood of more general support' might result in forcing a government over-reaction, thereby increasing revolutionary support among the people. Though Marighela achieved little success in his native Brazil, his teachings gave hope to other marginalized fringe revolutionary groups around the world. Through the use of seemingly senseless

violence against civilians, groups as diverse as the Red Brigades of Italy, the Irish Republican Army and the Palestine Liberation Organization sought to achieve wider political success.

From terror bombings on the streets of London to the hijacking of a French airliner to Entebee airport in Uganda, terrorists made their presence felt across the globe in the early 1970s. Working in small, tight-knit groups – often known as cells – the terrorists proved to be difficult intelligence targets. As the information age dawned, though, the job of tracking terrorists became infinitely more difficult as terrorist organizations began to multiply, expand and work together. Adding to the mounting anti-terrorist difficulties, several 'rogue' states – including Libya, Syria and Iran – began to offer terrorist groups shelter and supplies. With the protection of an established government, terrorists proved to be almost impossible to track down until they had already carried out their acts of violence. To counter terrorism, western nations have developed close ties between their law enforcement agencies and have sought more accurate intelligence regarding terrorist activities, often based on the pattern of success demonstrated by the Israeli Mossad. In addition, western

BELOW: Though the bombing campaign at the beginning of the war in Afghanistan provided television drama, the wonder weapons were not truly effective until infantry forces arrived in the area to act as the eyes and ears of the conflict.

nations have constructed quick-reaction specialist anti-terrorist forces, including the Counter Revolutionary Warfare Team of the British SAS and the American Delta Force. Essentially infantry-driven, these élite formations rely on training and initiative to overcome oftentimes desperate situations involving hundreds of hostages. Even so, as the struggle against terror continues, it has become apparent that the response to terror must be more broad based, and must involve more than simply a military solution.

Fuelled by fundamentalist Islam, several organizations in the Middle East, including Hezbollah and Islamic Jihad, sought to use terror to destroy Israel or aid Palestine, while other such organizations sought change within Arab nations more accurately to reflect their religious and societal views. Especially as the situation in Afghanistan worsened and American troops lingered in the Persian Gulf after the close of the conflict there, many fundamentalist Islamic groups began to isolate and pinpoint the United States as being the source which lurked behind many regional problems.

Utilizing modern, technological weaponry and communications, one terrorist group, known as al-Qaeda, began to construct an international terrorist network of previously unimagined size and sophistication. Headed by Saudi-born millionaire Osama bin Laden, who had fought in the conflict against the Soviets in Afghanistan, al-Qaeda worked patiently behind the scenes in several Arab nations, making use of societal implosion and anarchy to provide cover and recruits. The countries of Somalia and Afghanistan offered the best hope, and after Afghanistan fell under the rule of the fundamentalist Taliban régime, that nation even offered al-Qaeda overt support for the coming terrorist campaign against the United States.

'SEPTEMBER 11'

Though some of the al-Qaeda plots were discovered by western intelligence agencies, several more were not, illustrating the difficulties of fighting international terrorists who enjoy support from a nation. Several smaller strikes against US forces, from Mogadishu to an attack on the destroyer *Cole* in Yemen brought al-Qaeda and bin Laden into focus for the American intelligence community. Even so, US intelligence efforts were not enough to stop the most infamous terrorist attack ever. On 11 September 2001, al-Qaeda operatives, after years of training and planning,

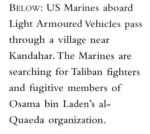

BELOW: US Marines aboard Light Armoured Vehicles pass through a village near Kandahar. The Marines are searching for Taliban fighters and fugitive members of Osama bin Laden's al-Quaeda organization.

LEFT: The US Department of Defense made a conscious decision in the 1970s to turn night into day. American fighting men possess a marked advantage over their less well-equipped foes, since infrared scopes, night-vision goggles and other low-light sensors enable them to fight effectively in pitch darkness.

hijacked four civilian airliners and used them as weapons against the US Pentagon and the twin towers of the World Trade Center in New York City. Succeeding beyond their wildest dreams, the attackers managed to collapse both of the World Trade Center towers and kill an estimated total of over 4000 people, at the same time causing untold economic damage that reverberated across the entire planet. Terrorism had reached a deadly new level of technical and technological expertise that induced worldwide horror, at the same time calling for a massive and innovative response.

AFGHAN INTERVENTION

With world backing and even somewhat reluctant support from the majority of Arab countries, the United States moved to attack the forces of al-Qaeda and their Taliban partners in Afghanistan. In the conflict, US forces had to overthrow the Taliban, thus defeating a nation at war, while also fighting an asymmetrical war against the elusive terrorists both in Afghanistan and in their bases around the world. The delicate situation called for US forces to wage war against an Islamic state and an Islamic terror group, and to retain the support of the Arab world lest the conflict spread and become a religious or ethnic war. Almost immediately, President George W. Bush, on the advice of Secretary of Defense

Donald Rumsfeld, ruled out the use of significant US ground forces as too provocative, choosing instead to rely on Afghan resistance fighters and a close alliance with Pakistan. While gathering air power with which to strike the Taliban government, the Bush administration also sent Special Forces units to the region to create and cement alliances with the disparate elements that formed the Afghan resistance, most notably the Northern Alliance. At the same time, diplomats and CIA operatives began close work with the Pakistanis in an effort to gather badly needed intelligence regarding the elusive network of al-Qaeda operatives.

BELOW: A Marine sniper stands guard at the major US base at Kandahar. Constant vigilance is essential in an anti-terror operation like 'Enduring Freedom', since there is very little difference between the appearance of Allied Afghans and those responsible for sheltering the organizers of the 11 September atrocities.

RIGHT: As the nature of warfare has become more complex, the training regimen of the modern infantryman has become more demanding, teaching soldiers to react and think quickly in the most confusing and dangerous situations. Here US soldiers use video cameras on their rifles to investigate a simulated urban environment.

ABOVE: Entering service with the US Army in 2001, the Land Warrior system is designed to use technology to enhance the fighting ability of the infantry soldier.

The military effort against the Taliban and al-Qaeda, dubbed 'Operation Enduring Freedom', began on 7 October 2001 and represented an unexpected mixture of military techniques. In part, the war was a traditional war against the forces of the Taliban government, involving fixed air and ground combat. However, the US in the main chose to fight the conflict by proxy.

In addition, though, the war represented an asymmetrical war against al-Qaeda terrorists, one which involved élite Special Forces and methods of counterinsurgency. The confusing military mix called for unprecedented

levels of integration on the part of the branches of the US military and intelligence community. At first it seemed that the War Against Terrorism would closely resemble the Gulf War, relying on the abilities of US air power to achieve victory. Bombers, ranging from high-flying B-52s to stealth aircraft, pounded Taliban and al-Qaeda positions with seemingly unerring accuracy. However, with a singular lack of intelligence concerning targeting in Afghanistan, the US air raids actually accomplished little.

It was not until élite Special Forces units entered Afghanistan that the war there began to change. In small groups, the Special Forces operatives fanned out into the Afghan countryside, adapting to their new situation by any means possible. Secretary Donald Rumsfeld in a recent speech stated that the Special Forces were operating in strained circumstances, that they 'rode horses – horses that had been trained to run into machine-gun fire, atop saddles that had been fashioned from wood and saddle bags that had been crafted from Afghan carpets. They used pack mules to transport equipment along some of the roughest terrain in the world, riding at night, in darkness, often near minefields and along narrow mountain trails with drops so sheer that, as one soldier put it, it took him a week to ease the death grip on his saddle.'

Operating in primitive conditions, the Special Forces relied on their most basic infantry skills: initiative reminiscent of troops on Omaha Beach and spirit and resiliency reminiscent of soldiers in World War I. The ultra-modern war had become a war reliant on well-trained soldiers on the ground, indicating that technology had changed little except the lethality of modern war. Linking up with Northern Alliance fighters, the Special Forces and their allies began to formulate their various plans of attack.

Using stealth, the Special Forces located the Taliban defensive emplacements near the critical town of Mazar-e-Sharif. On the appointed day of attack in early November the Special Forces neared the Taliban lines and designated targets for destruction by precision-guided munitions. Within two minutes the bombs began to strike with deadly accuracy, compromising the Taliban positions. In Rumsfeld's words next, 'hundreds of Afghan horsemen literally came riding out of the smoke, coming down on the enemy in clouds of dust and flying shrapnel. A few carried RPGs. Some had as little as 10 rounds for their weapons. And they rode boldly – Americans, Afghans, towards the Taliban and al-Qaeda fighters. It was the first cavalry attack of the 21st century.'

TALIBAN IN RETREAT
By 9 November Taliban resistance at Mazar-e-Sharif ceased and Northern Alliance troops, with their Special Forces advisers, seized the offensive across the country. Quickly the Taliban edifice crumbled, with their leadership admitting defeat in early December, leading to the formation of an interim Afghan Government under Hamid Karza. Though the struggle against terrorism continues and threatens to engulf other nations, the war in Afghanistan had come to a quick conclusion. The war in Afghanistan had represented a new blend of military techniques and technological levels of sophistication. Much reliance had been placed on the very latest western technology, from smart bombs to new earth-penetrating and thermobaric weapons for use against al-Qaeda cave networks. The coalition also made use of B-52 aircraft, a weapons system over 40 years old. However, the greatest reliance

in the war was placed upon men on the ground, and men on horseback. The blend of old and new styles of warfare was the key element of the campaign in Afghanistan, resulting in a devastating victory in an unexpected war.

TOWARDS THE FUTURE OF WAR
The conflicts of the post-Cold War era have left behind a confusing legacy. Will future conflicts closely resemble the Gulf War, as limited traditional wars seemingly dominated by technological weaponry? The experience of peacekeeping and peacemaking, though, might indicate that

BELOW: Land Warrior is the US Army's first fully integrated soldier fighting system. Through the helmet-mounted display, the soldier can view computer-generated graphical data, digital maps, intelligence information, troop locations and imagery from his weapon-mounted Thermal Weapon Sight (TWS) and video camera.

ABOVE: The role of infantry has changed much since 1900: today's infantryman must be a master of combat, peacemaking and technology.

RIGHT: Land Warrior's Computer/Radio Subsystem (CRS) combines radios and a Global Positioning System locator. A hand grip wired to the pack and attached to the soldier's chest acts as a computer mouse and also allows the wearer to change screens, key on the radio, change frequencies and send digital information. The software subsystem includes tactical and mission support modules, maps and tactical overlays, and the ability to capture and display video images from the soldier's weapon sight.

future wars will often take the form of brutal civil conflicts, struggles that pose great dangers to those who dare intervene, but possibly greater dangers if the world community simply stands aside.

Most recently terrorist attacks and rogue nations – with a lingering threat of a wider ethnic and religious conflict – seem to indicate an even more confusing military path towards the future.

The United States and its NATO Allies are now undergoing a series of military reforms, dubbed 'transformation' to make ready for the conflict of the future. Realizing that war in the 21st century can take a number of forms, the watchwords for transformation are 'flexibility' and 'integration'. The military must think ahead in an atmosphere of intellectual honesty towards a war that might take place in caves, in space, in a hostile rogue state, through renewed terrorist attacks on the home front, or in cyberspace. The US has made a number of changes in its defence policy, since the close of the Cold War demanding that its military be able to prosecute wars against two enemies simultaneously.

INTEGRATED WAR

Recent events, though, indicate that such a capability is rather redundant, and that the US should ready itself for a greater variety of conflicts rather than two traditional ones. As a result the US has

now dropped its two-war policy, and is in the process of reducing redundant weapons stockpiles, including reducing its nuclear capability. For American planners the era of Total War is over, as is the era of Limited War. Instead the world is making ready to embark on a period of what is termed as Integrated War.

In the new era of warfare brute strength and technological superiority will remain important but will represent only one facet of combat. US military planners believe, 'The ability of forces to communicate and operate seamlessly on the battlefield will be critical to our success. In Afghanistan, we saw composite teams of US Special Forces on the ground, working with Navy, Air Force and Marine pilots in the sky, to identify targets, communicate targeting information and coordinate the timing of strikes with devastating consequences for the enemy. The change between what we were able to do before US forces, Special Forces, were on the ground and after they were on the ground is absolutely dramatic. The lesson of this war is that effectiveness in combat will depend heavily on 'jointness', how well the different branches of our military can communicate and coordinate their efforts on the battlefield.'

Thus it seems that integration of forces, once called all-arms coordination, will be key to the multidimensional battlefield of the future. The infantryman, once nearly written off as a tool of future warfare unless fitted with a robotic exoskeleton, will continue to play the central role. The foot soldier's death knell has sounded many times, from the beginning of trench warfare to the introduction of the microchip. Still western armies will remain reliant upon the strength of their citizen soldiers. Highly trained and motivated, the infantryman has the most demanding job in the world. Trained in the use of brute force, he must also stand ready to show forbearance and patience as a humanitarian peacekeeper. Skilled in the most modern technology, he must be prepared to jettison the accoutrements of the technological age in favour of cold steel. While ready to call in precision-guided air strikes, the infantryman must be prepared to ride horseback through the Afghan desert. Much has changed in modern warfare, but battles are still won and lost by soldiers on the ground, and remain in the hands of the infantry.

ABOVE: Though some thought that technology had sounded the death knell for the foot soldier, recent conflicts shows that he still has an important role to play. Although his missions and equipment have become vastly more complex, it is still the infantryman who takes terrain and wins wars.

Index